Sunset
Casserole
Cook Book

By the Editors of Sunset Books
and Sunset Magazine

Lane Publishing Co.
Menlo Park, California

A boon to the busy cook...

Everyone's kitchen repertoire includes a favorite casserole, usually served when the cook runs out of ideas. But you'll never run out of ideas again after looking through the nearly 200 recipes we've included here.

You'll find hearty casseroles for pleasing hungry families; meatless entrées to delight a vegetarian; ethnic dishes with authentic flair; delectable casseroles tailored for the calorie-conscious; skillet meals that can be made in minutes; and easy side dishes that complete any menu.

Consider the endearing qualities of casseroles. Most can be prepared ahead of time; once in the oven, they free the cook from the kitchen; and they can, and should, be served to any number of people right in their original dish. What a boon to the busy cook who wants to serve a delicious meal without the flurry of last-minute preparation!

Edited by Linda Brandt

Special Consultant: Joan Griffiths
Assistant Editor,
Sunset Magazine

Photography: Nikolay Zurek

Photo Editor: Lynne B. Morrall

Design: Cynthia Hanson

Photo art: Darrow M. Watt

Cover: Veal scaloppine with teleme (page 28)
Photographed by Nikolay Zurek

Editor, Sunset Books: David E. Clark

First Printing September 1980

Contents

HEARTY FAVORITES   4
The ultimate in meat, poultry & seafood main dishes

MEATLESS ENTRÉES   32
Starring cheese, eggs & vegetables

ETHNIC CUISINE   44
International dishes with authentic flair

FOR THE CALORIE-CONSCIOUS   60
A sleek 450 calories (or fewer) per serving

STOVETOP SPECIALTIES   68
One-dish skillet meals, ready in minutes

SUPER SIDE DISHES   80
Vegetables & rice highlight these casseroles

INDEX   94

SPECIAL FEATURES
Garnishing tricks, step by step   14

Here are casseroles to please a crowd—& they're portable   28

Delectable sauces for the diet-conscious cook   65

Tips for freezing & transporting casseroles   76

Casserole breads...the container's the thing   86

Metric conversion table   96

HEARTY FAVORITES

The ultimate in meat, poultry & seafood main dishes

Savory Beef Stew

(Pictured on page 18)

Few dishes can rival the tempting flavor of a delicious, slow-cooked beef stew with vegetables. In our version, a hint of orange adds an unusual seasoning. Complete the menu with a loaf of crusty bread, such as three wheat casserole bread (page 87), and a salad of crisp greens.

    6 strips bacon, cut into 1-inch
         pieces
    2 to 2½ pounds boneless beef
         chuck, cut into 2-inch chunks
       Salt and pepper
    8 to 10 small white onions,
         peeled
    3 tablespoons all-purpose flour
 1½ cups dry red wine
    1 cup beef broth
    3 tablespoons brandy (optional)
    2 cloves garlic, minced or pressed
    1 strip (about 1 by 4 inches)
         orange peel
  ½ teaspoon *each* marjoram and
         thyme leaves
    1 medium-size onion studded
         with 6 whole cloves
    2 tablespoons butter or margarine
  ½ pound small mushrooms
    3 large carrots, diagonally sliced
         ½ inch thick
    3 to 4 tablespoons chopped
         parsley (optional)

In a wide frying pan over medium heat, cook bacon until browned and crumbly. With a slotted spoon, remove bacon from pan and place in a deep 3-quart casserole; reserve drippings. Sprinkle beef with salt and pepper; add to bacon drippings, a few pieces at a time, and cook, turning to brown on all sides. Remove from pan and place in casserole.

To pan juices, add white onions. Cook, shaking pan occasionally, until lightly browned. Remove from pan; reserve pan juices.

Stir flour into pan juices and cook until bubbly. Gradually pour in wine and broth and continue cooking and stirring until sauce boils and thickens. Add brandy (if desired), garlic, orange peel, marjoram, and thyme. Pour over beef in casserole. Tuck clove-studded onion down into liquid.

Bake, covered, in a 325° oven for 2½ hours. Meanwhile, in same frying pan over medium-high heat, melt butter. Add mushrooms and carrots and cook until juices have evaporated; set aside.

When stew has baked for 2½ hours, add browned onions, mushrooms, and carrots. Push them down into liquid, cover, and return to oven for 15 more minutes or until vegetables are tender.

Remove studded onion and sprinkle with parsley, if desired. Makes 6 servings.

Hearty Beef & Bean Stew

Consider this whole-meal stew whenever you have a hungry group to feed. Start with beans—either canned or, for greater economy, dried. Add beef shanks, onions, and tomatoes spiced with cumin, oregano, and garlic.

    2 tablespoons olive oil or salad oil
       About 2 pounds beef shank,
         cracked
    2 large onions, cut in thin
         lengthwise slices
    2 large cloves garlic, minced or
         pressed
    1 large can (28 oz.) tomatoes
 1½ teaspoons *each* salt, oregano
         leaves, and ground cumin
  ¼ teaspoon pepper
    1 cup water
       About 6 cups cooked or canned
         pink, pinto, or red beans,
         drained
       Thinly sliced green onion or
         chopped parsley

Heat oil in a 4 or 5-quart Dutch oven over medium heat. Add beef and cook, turning, until well browned; remove from pan.

To pan juices, add onions and garlic; cook, stirring, until onions are soft. Add tomatoes (break up with a spoon) and their liquid, salt, oregano, cumin, pepper, and water. Return meat to pan. Cover, reduce heat, and simmer for about 2 hours or until meat is very tender when pierced. Remove from heat.

Lift meat from pan and set aside to cool. Skim fat from pan, if needed, and add beans. Cut meat away from bone and into bite-size pieces; discard bone and gristle. Return meat to Dutch oven. (At this point you may cover and refrigerate until next day.)

Bake, covered, in a 350° oven for about 30 minutes (40 minutes, if refrigerated) or until heated through. Garnish each serving with green onion or parsley. Makes 6 to 8 servings.

Biscuit-topped Beef & Mushrooms

Biscuits lightened with sour cream bake on top of a rich beef and mushroom stew. To make the casserole ahead, simmer the beef until tender and refrigerate. Shortly before serving, reheat the beef, add sour cream, top with biscuits, then bake.

    2 to 4 tablespoons salad oil
 1½ to 2-pound boneless beef chuck
        roast, cut in ½-inch-thick
        strips about 2 inches long
    1 large onion, chopped
   ½ pound mushrooms, sliced
    1 can (14½ oz.) tomatoes
   ½ cup water
    1 can (6 oz.) tomato paste
    1 tablespoon sugar
 1½ teaspoons salt
   ½ teaspoon each Worcestershire
        and pepper
    2 tablespoons all-purpose flour
   ¾ cup sour cream
        Sour cream biscuits (recipe
        follows)

Heat 2 tablespoons of the oil in a 5-quart heat-resistant casserole or Dutch oven over medium-high heat. Add half the meat and cook until well browned; remove from pan. Add remaining meat and additional oil (if needed) and cook until well browned.

Return all meat to pan. Add onion and cook until soft. Stir in mushrooms, tomatoes (break up with a spoon) and their liquid, water, tomato paste, sugar, salt, Worcestershire, and pepper. Cover, reduce heat, and simmer for 1½ to 2 hours or until meat is very tender when pierced. (At this point you may cool, cover, and refrigerate until next day.)

Reheat if necessary before stirring flour into sour cream until blended; add to hot stew. Cook, stirring, until mixture thickens. Turn into a shallow 3-quart casserole or 9 by 13-inch baking dish. Prepare sour cream biscuits and arrange on hot stew. Bake, uncovered, in a 425° oven for about 25 minutes or until biscuits are well browned. Makes 6 servings.

Sour cream biscuits. Stir together 1¾ cups **all-purpose flour,** 2 teaspoons **baking powder,** and ½ teaspoon **salt.** With a pastry blender, cut in ½ cup **shortening** until fine crumbs form. Stir in ¾ cup **sour cream** until blended. On a floured board, pat dough into a ½-inch thickness. Cut biscuits in about 2-inch rounds.

Sicilian Beef & Vegetable Casserole

A vegetable-laden meat sauce combines with macaroni and spinach in this delicious hearty casserole. Since it's prepared in three stages, you may want to make the casserole a day in advance.

    1 tablespoon salad oil
 1½ pounds lean ground beef
    4 medium-size carrots, diced
    1 large onion, chopped
   ¼ pound mushrooms, sliced
    2 cans (6 oz. each) tomato paste
    1 can (1 lb.) tomatoes
   ⅔ cup dry sherry or water
 1½ teaspoons each salt, sugar, dry
        basil, and oregano leaves
   ½ teaspoon each pepper and garlic
        powder
    6 ounces elbow macaroni
        Boiling salted water
    1 package (10 oz.) frozen chopped
        spinach, thawed and drained
 1½ cups (6 oz.) shredded Cheddar
        cheese

Heat oil in a wide frying pan over medium heat. Add beef and cook until browned and crumbly. Remove with a slotted spoon and transfer to a 3-quart pan.

To pan drippings, add carrots, onion, and mushrooms; cook, stirring occasionally, for about 5 minutes. Add vegetables to meat along with tomato paste, tomatoes (break up with a spoon) and their liquid, sherry, salt, sugar, basil, oregano, pepper, and garlic powder. Reduce heat and simmer, uncovered, for about 30 minutes or until sauce thickens.

Cook macaroni in boiling salted water according to package directions. Drain well and combine with spinach. Spoon half the macaroni mixture into a lightly greased shallow 3-quart casserole or 9 by 13-inch baking dish. Top with half of the meat sauce and ½ cup of the cheese. Repeat layering, ending with remaining 1 cup cheese. (At this point you may cover and refrigerate until next day.)

(Continued on next page)

Bake, uncovered, in a 375° oven for 30 to 40 minutes (45 minutes, if refrigerated) or until heated through. Makes 6 to 8 servings.

Beef Cabbage Rolls with Sauerkraut

Hidden inside these plump cabbage rolls is a savory filling of ground beef, rice, catsup, and seasonings. But the real treat is the additional flavors of tangy sauerkraut and garlic sausage. A tomato sauce goes over all before baking.

1½ pounds lean ground beef
  1 large onion, finely chopped
  1 cup cooked rice
  ½ teaspoon salt
  ¼ teaspoon *each* pepper and
      paprika
  ¼ cup catsup
  1 clove garlic, minced or pressed
  ⅛ teaspoon liquid hot pepper
      seasoning
  1 large head cabbage (about
      3 lbs.)
      Boiling salted water
  1 quart sauerkraut, drained well
  1 pound kielbasa or other garlic
      sausage, cut in 1-inch pieces
  1 can (8 oz.) tomato sauce

In a wide frying pan over medium heat, cook beef until browned. Add onion and cook until soft. Discard fat. Stir in rice, salt, pepper, paprika, catsup, garlic, and hot pepper seasoning. Remove from heat and set aside.

Core cabbage and separate into leaves. Cut off and discard thickest portion of central rib from 16 large leaves (save remaining leaves for other uses). Place the 16 leaves in a large kettle of boiling salted water just long enough to blanch and soften them (about 1 minute); drain well.

In a shallow 4-quart casserole or Dutch oven, layer half the sauerkraut. Place about ¼ cup of the meat mixture at one end of each cabbage leaf, fold sides in over meat, and roll to enclose. Place each roll, seam side down, on sauerkraut.

Spoon any remaining meat mixture over the rolls. Add remaining sauerkraut, sausage chunks, and tomato sauce. (At this point you may cover and refrigerate until next day.)

Bake, covered, in a 350° oven for about 1½ hours or until casserole is steamy and flavors are well blended. Makes about 8 servings.

Yorkshire Relleno

Try this delightful combination of spicy meat and chili mixture topped with Yorkshire pudding for a quick-to-prepare supper that's a little out of the ordinary. You can adjust the heat level of this dish by varying the amount of chiles you use.

  1 pound lean ground beef or
      ground lamb
      Butter or margarine
  1 small onion, chopped
  1 clove garlic, minced or pressed
  2 teaspoons chili powder
  1 teaspoon *each* ground cumin
      and oregano leaves
  1 can (4 oz.) diced green chiles,
      drained
      Salt and pepper
  2 eggs
  1 cup *each* all-purpose flour and
      milk
  ½ teaspoon salt

Place a shallow 1½-quart casserole or 9-inch-square baking dish in the oven and preheat to 400°. Meanwhile, in a wide frying pan over medium heat, cook meat until well browned. Spoon drippings from meat into a measuring cup and add enough butter to make ¼ cup. Return drippings and butter to pan; add onion, garlic, chili powder, cumin, oregano, and chiles. Cook, stirring, until onion is soft. Season to taste with salt and pepper.

Beat eggs with flour, milk, and salt until smooth; set aside. Spread meat mixture evenly over bottom of hot casserole. Spoon flour mixture over top. Bake, uncovered, in a 400° oven for 25 to 30 minutes or until puffy and well browned. Makes 4 servings.

Oven Short Ribs with Noodles

In this beef and noodle dinner, all of the cooking takes place in the oven—including browning the meat. A fresh fruit salad and a crisp green vegetable complete the menu.

  3 pounds beef short ribs, cut in
      serving-size pieces
  ⅓ cup all-purpose flour
  1 teaspoon *each* salt and paprika
  ¼ teaspoon pepper
  2 cups hot water
  1 envelope (1½ oz.) dry onion
      soup mix
  6 ounces flat or twisted egg
      noodles
      Chopped parsley

Trim and discard excess fat from meat. In a small bag, combine flour, salt, paprika, and pepper. Place meat, a few pieces at a time, in bag and shake to coat completely. Arrange meat in a roasting pan or 9 by 13-inch baking dish. Bake, uncovered, in a 450° oven, turning meat occasionally, for about 20 minutes or until well browned.

Remove from oven and reduce temperature to 325°. Spoon off and discard fat from pan; add water and onion soup mix. Return to oven and bake, tightly covered, in a 325° oven for about 1½ to 2 hours or until meat is very tender when pierced.

Remove from oven and stir noodles into pan juices. Cover pan again and return to oven for 20 more minutes, stirring once or twice, or until noodles are tender. Sprinkle with parsley. Makes 4 to 6 servings.

Oven Sweet & Sour Pork

This sturdy entrée, combining boneless pork pieces and mixed dried fruit, is topped with a tangy sweet and sour sauce. Try serving it over hot buttered noodles or fluffy rice.

3½ pounds lean pork butt, boned
2 tablespoons salad oil
1 package (8 oz.) mixed dried fruit
1 cup chicken broth
½ cup apple juice
3 tablespoons lemon juice
1 tablespoon honey
2 tablespoons soy sauce
½ teaspoon garlic powder
¼ teaspoon *each* ground ginger and pepper
1 tablespoon cornstarch blended with 1 tablespoon water

Trim and discard excess fat from pork; cut meat into 1-inch cubes. Add oil to a broiler pan; set in oven while it preheats to 450°. Then add meat and bake, uncovered, stirring occasionally, for about 25 minutes or until meat is browned. Stir in fruit.

Combine broth, apple juice, lemon juice, honey, soy, garlic powder, ginger, and pepper; pour over meat. Reduce temperature to 350°. Bake, covered, for 40 minutes or until meat is tender when pierced.

With a slotted spoon, transfer meat and fruit to a platter; keep warm. Pour juices into a small pan; skim off and discard fat. Stir in cornstarch mixture and cook over medium-high heat, stirring, until sauce boils and thickens. Spoon over meat and fruit. Makes 6 servings.

Sausage-stuffed Pasta & Cheese

Tucked inside giant whole wheat or regular pasta shells is a delicious filling of browned sausage, cheese, parsley, and egg. The shells bake in an unusually flavorful tomato-mushroom sauce.

2 mild Italian sausages (3 oz. *each*)
1 egg
1 cup ricotta cheese
6 tablespoons grated Parmesan cheese
¼ teaspoon salt
1 tablespoon chopped parsley
2½ cups tomato-mushroom sauce (recipe follows)
12 whole wheat, spinach, or regular giant pasta shells, or 8 unfilled small manicotti
Boiling salted water

Remove casings from sausages. Crumble meat into a wide frying pan and cook over medium heat until browned. Discard drippings.

Beat egg into ricotta, then combine with sausage, 2 tablespoons of the Parmesan, salt, and parsley. Prepare tomato-mushroom sauce.

Cook pasta shells in boiling salted water just until *al dente* (still slightly firm). Drain, rinse with cold water, and drain again. Stuff with sausage-cheese mixture.

Spread half the tomato-mushroom sauce in a shallow 1½-quart casserole or 9-inch-square baking dish. Arrange filled pasta side by side in sauce. Spoon remaining sauce over top. (At this point you may cover and refrigerate until next day.)

Bake, covered, in a 350° oven for about 30 minutes (40 minutes, if refrigerated) or until bubbly and heated through. Sprinkle with remaining ¼ cup Parmesan. Makes about 4 servings.

Tomato-mushroom sauce. In a wide, deep frying pan or Dutch oven over medium heat, cook 6 strips **bacon** until crisp. Remove from pan, drain on paper towels, and crumble; set aside. Discard all but 3 tablespoons pan drippings. Add to drippings ½ pound sliced **mushrooms** and 1 clove **garlic** (minced or pressed); cook, stirring, until soft. Pour in 2 cans (about 1 lb. *each*) **Italian-style tomatoes** (break up with a spoon) and their liquid; stir. Add 1½ teaspoons **dry basil** and ¼ teaspoon **pepper**. Cook, uncovered, over medium-high heat for about 15 minutes or until sauce boils and thickens. Stir in bacon and season with **salt** to taste. Makes about 2½ cups.

Saffron Spaghetti Bake

Thick pork chops, browned in a skillet, rest atop a bed of tomato-flavored spaghetti mixed with sliced garlic sausages. Saffron gives the spaghetti mixture its bright yellow color. Saffron is expensive, though, so you might want to use turmeric instead.

4 tablespoons olive oil or salad oil
2 medium-size onions, chopped
2 cloves garlic, minced or pressed
3 medium-size tomatoes, peeled, seeded, and coarsely chopped
1 can (4 oz.) diced green chiles
1 tablespoon chopped parsley
2 beef bouillon cubes
¾ teaspoon salt
¼ teaspoon saffron or turmeric
1 quart boiling water
12 ounces spaghetti, broken in half
6 garlic sausages (about 1½ lbs.), peeled and sliced
6 loin pork chops (about 2 lbs.), cut ¾ inch thick
½ cup shredded Cheddar cheese

(Continued on next page)

Heat 3 tablespoons of the oil in a 4-quart pan over medium heat. Add onions and garlic and cook until onions are soft. Stir in tomatoes, chiles, parsley, bouillon cubes, salt, saffron, and water. Bring mixture to a boil. Add spaghetti and sausage. Cover, reduce heat, and simmer, stirring occasionally, for about 30 minutes or until most of the liquid is absorbed.

Meanwhile, in a wide frying pan over medium heat, brown chops on both sides in remaining 1 tablespoon oil. Turn spaghetti mixture into a lightly greased shallow 3-quart casserole or 9 by 13-inch baking dish. Arrange chops over spaghetti. (At this point you may cover and refrigerate until next day.)

Bake, covered, in a 350° oven for 45 minutes (1 hour, if refrigerated) or until pork is no longer pink near bone when slashed. Remove cover, sprinkle with cheese, and bake for a few minutes or until cheese melts. Makes 6 servings.

Lentils & Sausage Casserole

Lentils, part of the legume family, are high in protein and other nutrients, yet they're seldom seen on most American tables. In this casserole, fast-cooking lentils combine with mild Italian sausage in a vegetable-laced tomato sauce.

        12 ounces lentils
        4½ cups boiling water
         2 teaspoons salt
         1 clove garlic, minced or pressed
         1 pound mild Italian sausage
         1 large onion, coarsely chopped
      2 or 3 large carrots, diagonally sliced about ¼ inch thick
         1 can (8 oz.) tomato sauce
         3 tablespoons vinegar
            Minced parsley

Rinse lentils in water and drain well; discard any foreign material.

Place in a 4-quart casserole or Dutch oven; add boiling water, salt, and garlic. Cover and place in a 350° oven to begin baking.

Meanwhile, remove casings from sausage and cut into 1-inch chunks. In a wide frying pan over medium heat, cook sausage until well browned. Remove sausage and stir into lentils. Discard all but 2 tablespoons of the drippings; add onion to drippings and cook, stirring, until soft. Stir onion and carrots into lentils.

Bake, covered, for 45 minutes. Stir tomato sauce and vinegar into lentils and bake, uncovered, for 20 more minutes. Garnish with parsley. Makes about 6 servings.

Layered Spinach & Sausage Crêpes

Tender crêpes are layered like lasagne noodles in this main-dish casserole. Between crêpes, layers of spinach-cottage cheese mixture alternate with a sausage-flavored meat sauce. If you have some precooked crêpes in the freezer, the casserole goes together in minutes. You can then refrigerate the entire dish until time to bake. Our recipe for basic crêpes appears on page 56.

        12 crêpes (about 7 inches in diameter), at room temperature
         1 package (10 oz.) frozen chopped spinach, thawed
         1 pound mild Italian sausage
         1 large onion, chopped
        ¾ teaspoon *each* oregano leaves and dry basil
         1 jar (about 15 oz.) spaghetti sauce
         2 eggs
         1 pint (16 oz.) small-curd cottage cheese
         6 tablespoons grated Parmesan cheese

Squeeze out as much moisture as possible from thawed spinach; set aside. Remove casings and crumble sausage into a wide frying pan over medium heat. Cook, stirring,

until meat is lightly browned; discard drippings. Add onion and cook until soft. Stir in oregano, basil, and spaghetti sauce. Reduce heat and simmer, uncovered, stirring occasionally, for about 10 minutes or until sauce thickens.

Combine eggs, cottage cheese, spinach, and 4 tablespoons of the Parmesan cheese. In a lightly greased shallow 3-quart casserole or 9 by 13-inch baking dish, arrange 6 of the crêpes (overlap them slightly) so they cover the bottom of the casserole and come up the sides. Spread half the spinach mixture over crêpes; then half the meat sauce. Repeat layering with remaining crêpes, spinach, and meat sauce. Top with remaining Parmesan cheese. At this point you may cover and refrigerate until next day.

Bake, covered, in a 375° oven for 45 minutes (1 hour, if refrigerated) or until heated through. Let stand for about 15 minutes, then cut into squares to serve. Makes 6 to 8 servings.

Green Chile Strata & Sausage

Pork sausage, green chiles, and sharp Cheddar cheese bake together in layers in this rich custard dish. You can make it a day ahead because it needs to chill thoroughly in the refrigerator.

         1 pound lean bulk pork sausage
         5 slices firm white bread, lightly buttered and cut into ½-inch cubes
            Butter or margarine
         3 cups (12 oz.) shredded sharp Cheddar cheese
         1 can (4 oz.) diced green chiles, drained
         4 eggs
         2 cups milk
        ¾ teaspoon *each* salt and chili powder
        ¼ teaspoon pepper

In a large frying pan over medium heat, cook sausage until well browned. Discard fat and set meat aside.

Spread half the buttered bread cubes in a buttered shallow 2-quart casserole or 7 by 11-inch baking dish. Sprinkle with half the cheese and half the chiles. Add sausage and top with remaining bread cubes, cheese, and chiles.

Beat together eggs, milk, salt, chili powder, and pepper. Pour over bread mixture. Cover tightly and refrigerate for at least 8 hours, or until next day.

Bake, uncovered, in a 350° oven for about 1 hour or until golden brown and center of strata appears firm when casserole is gently shaken. Let stand for 10 to 15 minutes before serving. Makes about 6 servings.

Corned Beef Hash Casserole

Layers of corned beef hash, refried beans, browned sausage, and chile-flavored tomato sauce are crowned with two different cheeses before baking. Homemade or purchased tortilla chips and a salad of crisp greens round out the menu.

- 1 can (1 lb. 8 oz.) corned beef hash
- 1 can (16 oz.) refried beans
- 2 chorizo sausages (about 3 oz. each)
- 1 medium-size onion, chopped
- 1 can (8 oz.) tomato sauce
- 1 can (4 oz.) diced green chiles
- ¼ teaspoon oregano leaves
- 1½ cups (6 oz.) shredded jack cheese
- ½ cup grated Parmesan cheese

Spread hash in a shallow 2-quart casserole or 9-inch-square baking dish. Cover evenly with beans and set aside.

Remove and discard casings from chorizos; chop sausage. In a wide frying pan over medium heat, cook sausage until crumbly; add onion and cook until soft.

Drain and discard drippings, if any, and add tomato sauce, chiles, and oregano. Pour sauce over beans, top with jack cheese, and spinkle evenly with Parmesan. (At this point you may cover and refrigerate until next day.)

Bake, uncovered, in a 375° oven for 30 minutes (40 minutes, if refrigerated) or until bubbly and heated through. Makes 6 to 8 servings.

Ham & Pea Pasta Ramekins

Give pizazz to individual ramekins filled with Swiss cheese and fancy-shaped pasta by adding tiny green peas, julienne ham strips, sliced mushrooms, and toasted almonds.

- ¼ cup sliced almonds
- 3 tablespoons butter or margarine
- ¼ pound each mushrooms (thinly sliced) and cooked ham (cut into julienne strips)
- 1 package (10 oz.) frozen tiny peas, thawed
- 2 tablespoons all-purpose flour
- 1½ cups each milk and half-and-half (light cream)
- 1 cup (4 oz.) shredded Swiss cheese
- 12 ounces medium-size, fancy-shaped macaroni (such as mostaccioli or conchiglie)
  Boiling salted water

Spread almonds in a shallow pan and toast in a 350° oven for about 8 minutes or until lightly browned.

In a wide frying pan over medium-high heat, melt 1 tablespoon of the butter. Add mushrooms and cook until soft. Add ham and continue cooking until most of the liquid has evaporated. Remove from heat, stir in peas, and set aside.

In a 3-quart pan over medium heat, melt remaining 2 tablespoons butter. Blend in flour and cook, stirring, until bubbly. Gradually pour in milk and half-

and-half and continue cooking and stirring until sauce boils and thickens. Remove from heat and stir in cheese.

Cook macaroni in boiling salted water according to package directions. Drain well and combine with ham mixture. Spoon into 6 lightly greased ramekins (about 2-cup size) and top with cheese sauce. Sprinkle with almonds. (At this point you may cover and refrigerate until next day.)

Bake, covered, in a 350° oven for 12 to 15 minutes (20 minutes, if refrigerated) or until heated through. Makes 6 servings.

Ham, Spinach & Brown Rice

Here's a tempting casserole chock-full of nutritious ingredients: brown rice, roasted sunflower seeds, spinach, jack and Cheddar cheese, mushrooms, marinated artichoke hearts, and ham.

- 2½ cups water
- ½ teaspoon salt
- 1 cup brown rice
- 2 tablespoons salad oil
- ½ pound mushrooms, sliced
- ½ cup chopped green onions (including tops)
- ¼ cup salted roasted sunflower seeds
- 2 packages (10 oz. each) frozen chopped spinach, thawed
- ¾ cup shredded jack cheese
- 1 to 2 cups cooked ham, cut into 1-inch cubes
- 1 jar (6 oz.) marinated artichoke hearts, drained
- ¾ cup shredded Cheddar cheese

(Continued on next page)

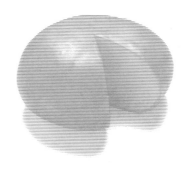

In a 1-quart pan, bring water and salt to a boil. Add rice; then cover, reduce heat, and simmer for 45 minutes or until tender to bite. Remove from heat, uncover, and cool slightly.

Meanwhile, heat oil in a wide frying pan over medium heat. Add mushrooms and green onions and cook until soft; set aside. With a fork, mix sunflower seeds into rice and spread evenly in a lightly greased shallow 2-quart casserole or 9-inch-square baking dish. Over rice mixture, layer spinach, then jack cheese, then ham. Spread mushroom mixture over ham and arrange artichokes on top. Sprinkle with Cheddar cheese. (At this point you may cover and refrigerate until next day.)

Bake, covered, in a 350° oven for about 30 minutes (40 minutes, if refrigerated) or until mixture is bubbly and cheese is melted. Makes about 6 servings.

Beef Tongue Creole

Tongue, in almost any form, has never been very popular in American kitchens. If you've hesitated to serve beef tongue, try this unusual version featuring thin slices of tender meat simmered in a rich vegetable sauce.

1 smoked beef tongue (3½ to 4 lbs.)
2 tablespoons butter or margarine
2 tablespoons all-purpose flour
1 can (28 oz.) Italian-style tomatoes
½ cup chopped parsley
1 medium-size onion, chopped
1 medium-size green pepper, seeded and chopped
1 cup chopped celery (including tops)
1 medium-size carrot, shredded
8 cloves garlic, minced or pressed
2 teaspoons dry basil
1 tablespoon Worcestershire
2 tablespoons catsup
4 tablespoons dry sherry
1 teaspoon *each* pepper, caraway seeds, thyme leaves, oregano leaves, and dill weed

Place tongue in a 5-quart kettle or Dutch oven. Cover with water and bring to a boil. Reduce heat; cover and simmer for about 3 hours or until tongue is very tender when pierced. Cool in broth, then lift out tongue and set aside. Taste liquid, and if not too salty, reserve 1 cup; if too salty, discard all liquid. Remove and discard skin and tubes from tongue; cut tongue into ½-inch-thick slices.

In a 3-quart pan over medium heat, melt butter. Blend in flour and cook, stirring, until bubbly. Gradually add reserved broth (or 1 cup water) and continue cooking and stirring until sauce boils and thickens. Add tomatoes (break up with a spoon) and their liquid, parsley, onion, green pepper, celery, carrot, garlic, basil, Worcestershire, catsup, sherry, pepper, caraway, thyme, oregano, and dill. Bring to a boil, then remove from heat.

Arrange sliced tongue in a shallow 3-quart casserole or 9 by 13-inch baking dish. Spoon sauce over slices.

Bake, uncovered, in a 300° oven for about 1½ hours, stirring several times, or until sauce is thickened. Arrange tongue slices on a warm platter. Spoon some of the sauce over tongue; pour remaining sauce in a bowl to pass at the table. Makes 6 to 8 servings.

Crusty Fettucine Puff

Fettucine, the ribbon-shaped pasta noodles, combine with chopped ham, Swiss and Parmesan cheeses, egg yolks, and beaten egg whites in this lightly puffed, oven-browned casserole. Serve small portions for a first course as the Italians do, or offer it as a lunch or supper entrée accompanied by a salad of crisp greens. Look for fresh fettucine noodles in the refrigerated section of your market.

1 package (about 10 oz.) fresh fettucine
Boiling salted water
½ cup butter or margarine, cut in pieces
½ pound cooked ham, finely chopped
1¼ cups *each* shredded Swiss cheese and grated Parmesan cheese
1¾ cups milk, scalded
Dash of pepper
⅛ teaspoon ground nutmeg
7 eggs
Butter or margarine

Cook noodles in boiling salted water according to package directions until just barely tender (about 2 minutes). Drain well and place in a large bowl. Add the ½ cup butter, ham, Swiss and Parmesan cheeses, milk, pepper, and nutmeg. With a large fork and spoon, gently toss together until well combined. Let cool for as long as 1 hour.

Separate eggs. Gently stir egg yolks into noodle mixture. Beat egg whites just until stiff, moist peaks form. Fold egg whites, a portion at a time, into noodle mixture just until blended. Transfer to a buttered 2½ to 3-quart soufflé dish or deep casserole.

Bake, uncovered, in a 350° oven for 40 minutes. Raise oven temperature to 450° and bake for about 10 more minutes or until top is well browned. Makes 12 to 14 servings as a first course, 6 to 8 servings as a main dish.

Layered Chile Chicken & Tortillas

Diced green chiles and chili powder give this Mexican-style chicken dish zest and pungency. Serve it with a cooling salad of mixed greens and sliced oranges or perhaps a side dish of baked refried beans.

- 2 tablespoons salad oil
- 2 large onions, coarsely chopped
- 2 cloves garlic, minced or pressed
- 2 teaspoons *each* chili powder, dry basil, and salt
- 1 tablespoon sugar
- ½ teaspoon oregano leaves
- 1 can (4 oz.) diced green chiles, drained
- 2 cans (15 oz. *each*) tomato sauce
- 1 cup chicken broth
- 12 corn tortillas
  Salad oil
- 4 cups shredded cooked chicken
- 4 cups (1 lb.) shredded Cheddar cheese
  Sour cream (optional)

Heat the 2 tablespoons oil in a wide frying pan over medium heat. Add onions and garlic and cook, stirring, until onions are soft. Stir in chili powder, basil, salt, sugar, oregano, green chiles, tomato sauce, and chicken broth. Bring to a boil. Reduce heat and simmer for 10 minutes.

Meanwhile, soften tortillas by heating a very small amount of oil (about ½ teaspoon) in a small frying pan over medium-high heat. When oil is hot, add tortillas, one at a time, and spin them with your fingers; turn tortillas over and repeat for other side. Add additional oil, in very small amounts, as needed. As tortillas are softened, stack them and set aside.

To assemble casserole, line the bottom of a greased shallow 3-quart casserole or 9 by 13-inch baking dish with 6 of the tortillas, overlapping them slightly. Add half the chicken, half the sauce, and half the cheese. Arrange remaining tortillas and repeat layering of ingredients, ending with cheese. (At this point you may cool, cover, and refrigerate until next day.)

Bake, uncovered, in a 350° oven for 40 minutes or until casserole is heated through. (If refrigerated, bake, covered, for 1 hour; then uncover and bake for 15 more minutes.) Spoon sour cream over individual servings, if desired. Makes 6 to 8 servings.

Fila Chicken & Artichoke Casserole

(Pictured on page 31)

Flaky, golden, paper-thin sheets of fila dough make an impressive and savory casserole when layered with creamed chicken and another creamy mixture of artichokes, mushrooms, and rice. Look for fila in the freezer or refrigerator section of your market. If frozen, thaw fila according to package instructions. Since working with fila can be a little tricky at first (it dries out quickly), have all your ingredients at hand when it's time to assemble the casserole.

- Poached chicken (recipe follows)
- About ¾ cup butter or margarine
- ¼ cup all-purpose flour
- ½ cup half-and-half (light cream) or whipping cream
- ½ teaspoon *each* salt and white pepper
- 2 cloves garlic, minced or pressed
- 1 large onion, chopped
- ½ pound mushrooms, sliced
- ¾ cup rice
- 1½ cups chicken broth
- ¾ teaspoon summer savory
- 1 package (9 oz.) frozen artichoke hearts, thawed
- 14 to 16 sheets fila dough (if frozen, thaw according to package directions)

Prepare poached chicken.

In a medium-size pan over medium heat, melt ¼ cup of the butter. Blend in flour and cook, stirring, until bubbly. Gradually pour in 2 cups chicken-poaching stock and half-and-half; continue cooking and stirring until sauce boils and thickens. Stir in salt and pepper and set aside.

In a 2-quart pan over medium heat, melt 3 tablespoons of the butter. Add garlic, onion, and mushrooms and cook until vegetables are soft. Stir in rice, coating lightly with butter. Add broth and savory; bring to a boil. Cover, reduce heat, and simmer for 20 minutes or until all liquid is absorbed. Stir in artichokes, cover, and continue simmering for 5 more minutes. Stir in 1 cup of the cream sauce; set aside to cool. To the remaining cream sauce, add poached chicken pieces.

Melt remaining 5 tablespoons butter; brush some on bottom and sides of a 9 by 13-inch baking dish. Stack fila sheets and keep covered with plastic wrap while you work.

Place 1 sheet fila in bottom of pan, folding to fit; brush lightly with melted butter. Repeat with 6 or 7 more sheets, lightly brushing each sheet with butter. Spread half the rice mixture over fila; layer chicken in cream sauce over rice. Top with remaining rice. Cover with remaining fila, folding edges under to fit pan; lightly brush

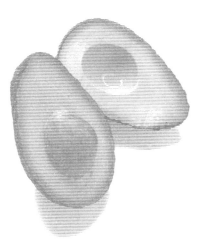

each sheet with butter. Tuck top sheet down inside of pan; brush lightly with butter.

With a sharp knife, score top 3 or 4 fila layers to mark 8 to 12 pieces. (At this point you may cover and refrigerate until next day.)

Bake, uncovered, in a 350° oven for about 45 minutes (60 to 70 minutes, if refrigerated) or until golden brown and heated through. Makes 8 to 12 servings.

Poached chicken. You'll need 1 **broiler-fryer chicken** (3 to 3½ lbs.), cut in pieces, plus 1 whole **chicken breast** (about 1 lb.). Split all breast pieces and set aside. Place remaining chicken in a 5-quart pan and add 1 cup dry **white wine**, 1½ teaspoons *each* **salt** and **thyme leaves**, 1 **bay leaf**, ¾ teaspoon dry **rosemary**, and 2 cups **water**. Bring to a boil. Cover, reduce heat, and simmer for 25 minutes. Add breast pieces, cover, and continue simmering for 20 more minutes or until meat near bone is no longer pink when slashed. Lift out chicken (reserve stock) and let cool. Remove skin and bones and tear meat into bite-size pieces. Skim off and discard fat from stock. Boil stock, uncovered, until reduced to 2 cups. Remove bay leaf.

Lattice-topped Chicken Pie

(Pictured on page 23)

Concealed beneath a golden, lattice-style crust are chunks of tender chicken and three vegetables enveloped in a rich cream sauce. Directions for lattice-style crust appear on page 15. If you want to simplify the crust, just use a single round of pastry and flute the edge.

- 4 tablespoons butter or margarine
- ½ pound mushrooms, sliced
- 2 medium-size carrots, sliced ¼ inch thick
- 2 tablespoons all-purpose flour
- 1½ cups chicken broth
- ½ cup milk
- 1 tablespoon *each* Worcestershire and grated lemon peel
- 2 egg yolks
- ½ cup half-and-half (light cream) Salt and pepper
- 4 to 5 cups cooked chicken, torn into bite-size pieces
- 1 package (10 oz.) frozen peas, thawed Pastry for a double-crust 9-inch pie
- 1 egg, lightly beaten

In a wide frying pan over medium heat, melt 2 tablespoons of the butter. Add mushrooms and carrots and cook until mushrooms are soft. Melt remaining 2 tablespoons butter. Blend in flour and cook, stirring, until bubbly. Gradually pour in chicken broth and milk and continue cooking and stirring until sauce boils and thickens. Add Worcestershire and lemon peel. Beat egg yolks with the ½ cup half-and-half; add to sauce and remove from heat. Season to taste with salt and pepper. Combine chicken and peas and turn into a 2½-quart casserole. Spoon sauce over chicken.

Roll out pastry and cut into ½-inch-wide strips. Starting in center of pie, weave strips into lattice pattern as directed on page 15. Reserve excess pastry dough for other uses. (Or, roll out pastry for

1 pie crust, cover casserole with dough, and flute edge or decorate top, as desired. Cut several slits in crust.) Brush crust thoroughly with beaten egg.

Bake in a 425° oven for about 25 minutes or until crust is golden brown and pie is heated through. Makes 4 to 6 servings.

Chicken, Mushroom & Artichoke Casserole

Here is an elegant casserole: chicken breasts covered with artichoke hearts as well as mushrooms in a sherry-flavored wine sauce. Best of all—it can be completed in advance.

- 4 whole chicken breasts (about 1 lb. *each*), split Salt, pepper, and paprika
- 2 tablespoons *each* butter or margarine and salad oil
- 2 packages (9 oz. *each*) frozen artichoke hearts, thawed
- ¼ pound mushrooms, thinly sliced
- 3 tablespoons all-purpose flour
- 1 cup chicken broth
- ¼ cup dry sherry
- ¼ teaspoon dry rosemary Chopped parsley

Lightly sprinkle chicken breasts with salt, pepper, and paprika. Heat butter and oil in a wide frying pan over medium heat. Add chicken, a few pieces at a time, and cook until well browned. Transfer chicken (reserve pan juices) to a shallow 3-quart casserole or 9 by 13-inch baking dish. Cover chicken with artichoke hearts. To the reserved pan juices, add mushrooms and cook over medium heat until soft. Blend in flour and cook, stirring, until bubbly. Gradually pour in chicken broth and sherry and continue cooking and stirring until sauce boils and thickens. Add rosemary. Spoon sauce over chicken. (At this point you may cool, cover, and refrigerate until next day.)

Bake, covered, in a 375° oven

for 30 minutes (40 to 45 minutes, if refrigerated) or until meat near bone is no longer pink when slashed. Garnish with chopped parsley. Makes 6 to 8 servings.

Chicken Breasts in Orange Sauce

Succulent chicken breasts and tangy orange juice make a winning combination in this easy, make-ahead casserole. Hot buttered rice, a green salad, and fresh fruit for dessert complete the menu.

  ⅓ cup all-purpose flour
  1 teaspoon *each* salt and paprika
    Dash of pepper
    Dash of garlic powder
  3 whole chicken breasts (about 1 lb. *each*), split
  6 tablespoons salad oil
  ¼ pound mushrooms, quartered
  2 cups diagonally sliced carrots, cut ½ inch thick
  1 can (10¾ oz.) condensed cream of mushroom soup
  ½ cup *each* orange juice and dry white wine (or 1 cup orange juice)
  ¼ teaspoon ground nutmeg
  2 teaspoons brown sugar

In a small bag, combine flour, salt, paprika, pepper, and garlic powder. Place chicken pieces, a few at a time, in bag and shake to coat completely.

Heat oil in a wide frying pan over medium heat. Add chicken, a few pieces at a time, and cook until well browned. Transfer chicken to a shallow 3-quart casserole or 9 by 13-inch baking dish. Scatter mushrooms and carrots over top. Mix soup, orange juice, wine, nutmeg, and brown sugar until smooth; spoon over chicken. (At this point you may cool, cover, and refrigerate until next day.)

Bake, covered, in a 350° oven for 30 minutes (40 to 45 minutes, if refrigerated) or until meat near bone is no longer pink when slashed. Makes 4 to 6 servings.

Chicken & Broccoli Mornay

Vivid green broccoli contrasts with prosciutto-wrapped boneless chicken breasts covered with a nutmeg-flavored cheese sauce. Both the chicken breasts and the tender-crisp broccoli can be prepared well in advance.

  2 cups chicken broth
  3 whole chicken breasts (about 1 lb. *each*), split
  2 pounds broccoli
  6 tablespoons *each* butter or margarine and all-purpose flour
  1½ cups half-and-half (light cream) or milk
  ¼ cup shredded Swiss cheese
  2 tablespoons grated Parmesan cheese
  ¼ teaspoon ground nutmeg
    Salt and pepper
  6 thin slices prosciutto or cooked ham
  ⅓ cup grated Parmesan cheese
    Paprika

Heat broth in a 2 or 3-quart pan over medium heat; add chicken. Cover, reduce heat, and simmer for 15 minutes. Remove chicken (reserve broth) and cool. Keeping each half breast in one piece, carefully remove bones and skin (reserve both); set aside.

Return bones and skin to broth. Cover and simmer for 30 more minutes. Discard bones and skin; skim and discard fat. You should have about 1¾ cups broth (or boil longer to reduce, if necessary); set aside.

Meanwhile, rinse broccoli; discard leaves and coarse outer layer from stems. Slice stems crosswise about ¼ inch thick and cut flowers into equal branches. Steam broccoli over boiling water until just tender-crisp (about 5 minutes). Chill quickly by plunging broccoli into cold water; then drain and set aside.

In a wide frying pan over medium heat, melt butter. Blend in flour and cook, stirring, until bubbly. Gradually pour in reserved broth and half-and-half and continue cooking and stirring until sauce boils and thickens. Add Swiss cheese and the 2 tablespoons Parmesan cheese; stir until cheese melts. Add nutmeg and salt and pepper to taste.

To assemble casserole, scatter broccoli stems in a well-greased shallow 3-quart casserole or 9 by 13-inch baking dish. Group broccoli branches at each end of dish. Wrap a slice of prosciutto around each chicken breast and arrange in center of dish. Spoon sauce over chicken only. Top with the ⅓ cup Parmesan cheese and sprinkle lightly with paprika. (At this point you may cool, cover, and refrigerate until next day.)

Bake, uncovered, in a 350° oven for about 30 minutes (40 to 45 minutes, if refrigerated) or until heated through. Makes 6 servings.

Tarragon Chicken

Your family will rave about the flavor of this delicious casserole, and you'll appreciate how quickly it goes together. Just top pieces of chicken with chopped onion, seasonings, and canned soup. For a simple but attractive garnish, sprinkle almonds on top.

  3 whole chicken breasts (about 1 lb. *each*), split, or 1 broiler-fryer (3 to 3½ lbs.), cut in pieces
  2 medium-size onions, coarsely chopped
  1½ teaspoons dry tarragon
  1 teaspoon salt
  ¼ teaspoon *each* poultry seasoning and pepper
  1 can (10¾ oz.) condensed cream of chicken soup
  ¼ cup milk
  ¼ cup sliced or slivered almonds

Arrange chicken, skin side up, in a shallow 3-quart casserole or 9 by 13-inch baking dish. Sprinkle onions, tarragon, salt, poultry seasoning, and pepper over chicken.

(Continued on page 16)

Garnishing tricks, step by step

A touch of color, an unusual shape, or just a careful arrangement of ingredients can transform an ordinary-looking casserole into something special. And as impressive as they look, many garnishes require only a few minutes and a soupçon of skill.

Decorate the top of your casserole with vegetables and fruits cut into fancy shapes with special utensils available in gourmet shops and in the cookware section of most department stores. We illustrate how to create these designs with carrots, tomatoes, mushrooms, bell peppers, and lemons.

Additional instructions explain how to pipe mashed potatoes around a casserole's edge, design a tomato rose, and weave a lattice-style crust.

Fancy-shaped Vegetables

Hors d'oeuvre cutters create fancy shapes from carrots and other firm vegetables.

Ripple-edge knife cuts carrots and other firm vegetables into decorative sticks.

Channel knife scores tops of mushrooms with just the slightest amount of pressure.

Lemon Accents

Channel knife scores surface of lemon when you apply firm pressure; then slice lemon in desired thickness.

Zigzag cut made with small, sharp knife divides lemon in half; use as is, or scoop out pulp and fill shell with sauce or dressing.

Cut lemon slice once from outer edge to center; twist into S-shape and add parsley sprig.

Tomato Roses

Place small firm tomato in boiling water for about 1 minute, then plunge into cold water. Imagine a ½-inch-wide circle on bottom of tomato. With sharp knife, carefully cut most of the way around and then beneath circle; peel tomato in one continuous piece with circle still attached.

After peeling tomato completely, carefully scrape any excess pulp off skin. Roll up tightly, pulp side in, ending at circle. Twist gently to make rose stand on circle.

Flare edges of rose slightly. Arrange completed roses on casserole or individual plates and add parsley sprig.

Potato Piping

Fancy-shaped tips, used in cake decorating for special effects, are fitted onto pastry bag filled with seasoned mashed potato.

Use one hand to squeeze end of bag closed and force potato out through tip. Other hand guides bag around edge of dish. Casserole should be completely baked and still hot.

When piping is completed, return casserole to 375° oven for about 5 minutes or until brown and crusty (or broil 5 inches from heat for about 1 minute).

Lattice-style Crust

Prepare enough pastry for two crusts. Roll out half the crust, about ⅛ inch thick. With pizza cutter or sharp knife, cut strips of dough in desired width. Repeat with remaining crust.

Beginning in center of pie, lay several strips in one direction, fairly close together. Over them, lay several strips in opposite direction; weave in over-under-over manner.

Complete weaving and trim excess dough, leaving about ½-inch overlap. Tuck overlap inside dish or crimp edges. Bake according to recipe.

Combine soup and milk; spoon over chicken. (At this point you may cover and refrigerate until next day.)

Bake, uncovered, in a 375° oven for 30 minutes for breasts or 40 minutes for chicken pieces (40 to 55 minutes, if refrigerated). Sprinkle casserole with almonds and bake for 10 more minutes or until meat near bone is no longer pink when slashed. Makes 4 to 6 servings.

Crab-stuffed Chicken Breasts

For a special dinner or buffet, what could be more imaginative than these stuffed chicken breasts? The very thin, boned breasts are filled with a delicious crab and parsley mixture, then rolled up and baked in a mushroom sauce.

  4 **whole chicken breasts (about 1 lb. *each*), split, boned, and skinned**
  ¼ **cup butter or margarine**
  ½ **cup thinly sliced green onions (including tops)**
  ¼ **pound mushrooms, thinly sliced**
  3 **tablespoons all-purpose flour**
  ¼ **teaspoon thyme leaves**
  ½ **cup *each* chicken broth, milk, and dry white wine**
     Salt and pepper
  ½ **pound cooked fresh or canned crab**
  ⅓ **cup *each* finely chopped parsley and fine dry bread crumbs**
  1 **cup (4 oz.) shredded Swiss cheese**

Place each chicken breast between 2 sheets of plastic film on a cutting board. With a mallet, pound breasts until each is about ¼ inch thick; set aside.

In a wide frying pan over medium heat, melt butter. Add onions and mushrooms and cook until soft. Blend in flour and thyme and cook, stirring, until bubbly. Gradually pour in broth, milk, and wine and continue cooking and stirring until sauce boils and thickens. Season to taste with salt and pepper.

In a small bowl, stir together ¼ cup of the sauce, crab, parsley, and bread crumbs. Divide mixture among chicken breasts; fold edges up and over mixture; roll up tightly into a bundle. Place bundles, seam side down, in a lightly greased shallow 3-quart casserole or 9 by 13-inch baking dish. Spoon remaining sauce over chicken and sprinkle with cheese. (At this point, you may cover and refrigerate until next day.)

Bake, covered, in a 400° oven for about 40 minutes (50 minutes, if refrigerated) or until meat is no longer pink when slashed. Makes 4 to 8 servings.

Cheese-topped Chicken with Asparagus

Prepare these chicken breasts ahead, place them in individual ramekins, then serve them bubbly-hot for a special brunch or afternoon luncheon. The boneless breasts are pounded wafer thin, covered with a slice of ham, topped with mozzarella cheese, and placed over asparagus spears.

  2 **whole chicken breasts (about 1 lb. *each*), split, skinned, and boned**
  ¼ **cup all-purpose flour**
  ½ **teaspoon salt**
  ¼ **teaspoon pepper**
  1 **egg, lightly beaten**
     About 2 tablespoons *each* butter and salad oil
  1 **pound asparagus, ends trimmed**
  4 **thin slices (about ¼ lb.) cooked ham**
  4 **thin slices (about ¼ lb.) mozzarella cheese**

Place each chicken breast between 2 sheets of plastic film on a cutting board. With a mallet, pound breasts until each is about ⅜ inch thick.

In a small bag, combine flour, salt, and pepper. Dip chicken in egg, then place chicken, a few pieces at a time, in bag and shake to coat completely.

Heat 1 tablespoon *each* of the butter and oil in a wide frying pan over medium heat. Cook half the chicken, turning pieces, until lightly browned (about 1½ minutes on a side). Repeat with remaining chicken, adding more butter and oil, if needed.

Meanwhile, steam asparagus over boiling water until just tender-crisp (about 5 to 7 minutes). Arrange asparagus in 4 shallow ramekins (1½ or 2-cup size). In each, place 1 chicken breast, 1 slice of ham, and 1 slice of cheese on top. (At this point you may cool, cover, and refrigerate until next day.)

Bake, covered, in a 375° oven for about 15 minutes (30 minutes, if refrigerated) or until heated through. Makes 4 servings.

Chicken Dijon

Butter-browned and brandy-flamed pieces of chicken are baked in a golden, rich cream sauce with the delicious flavor of Dijon mustard.

  ⅓ **cup all-purpose flour**
  ¾ **teaspoon salt**
  ¼ **teaspoon pepper**
  6 **each chicken legs and thighs (about 3 lbs. *total*)**
  4 **tablespoons butter or margarine**
  2 **tablespoons brandy**
  1 **small onion, finely chopped**
  ¼ **cup minced parsley**
  2 **tablespoons *each* Dijon mustard and lemon juice**
  2 **cups whipping cream**
  3 **egg yolks, lightly beaten**
     Salt
     Chopped parsley

In a small bag, combine flour, salt, and pepper. Place chicken, a few pieces at a time, in a bag and shake to coat completely. In a wide frying pan over medium heat, melt butter. Add chicken, a few pieces at a time, and cook until well browned on all sides. Return all chicken to pan.

In a small pan, warm brandy and set aflame; immediately pour over chicken, shaking pan until flame dies. Lift chicken from pan (reserve pan juices) and transfer to a shallow 3-quart casserole or 9 by 13-inch baking dish.

To pan juices, add onion and minced parsley and cook over medium heat until onion is soft (about 4 minutes). Blend in mustard, lemon juice, and whipping cream. Bring to a boil, stirring, and spoon over chicken. (At this point you may cool, cover, and refrigerate until next day.)

Bake, covered, in a 375° oven for 45 minutes (55 minutes, if refrigerated), or until thigh meat near bone is no longer pink when slashed.

Drain (or siphon) cooking sauce from casserole and place in a wide frying pan. Boil for 1 minute. Blend some of the hot liquid into egg yolks, then return mixture to pan. Reduce heat to low and cook, stirring constantly, until sauce thickens (*do not boil*). Season to taste with salt. Spoon sauce over chicken and sprinkle with chopped parsley. Makes 6 servings.

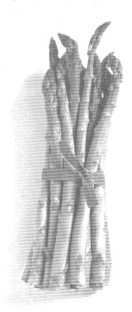

Savory Chicken in White Wine

White wine replaces the conventional red wine in this delicious version of the famed coq au vin. The dish combines browned chicken pieces and coarsely chopped bacon, as well as carrots, onions, and mushroom caps.

    2 broiler-fryer chickens (3 to
          3½ lbs. *each*), cut in pieces
    ½ teaspoon salt
    6 slices bacon, coarsely chopped
    2 tablespoons butter or margarine
    3 large carrots, diagonally sliced
          ½ inch thick
       Boiling salted water
    ¼ cup finely chopped shallots or
          green onions (including tops)
    12 small white onions, peeled
    2 cups dry white wine
    1 pound medium-size
          mushrooms, stems removed
    2 tablespoons cornstarch blended
          with 2 tablespoons water

Sprinkle chicken pieces evenly with salt. In a 12 to 14-inch frying pan (or one large enough to hold all the chicken) over medium heat, cook bacon until crisp. Remove bacon from pan; drain, crumble, and set aside.

To pan drippings, add butter and melt. Add chicken, a few pieces at a time, and cook until well browned on all sides. Pour off pan drippings. Return all chicken to pan.

Meanwhile, cook carrots in a small amount of boiling salted water for 5 minutes; drain well. Add to browned chicken along with shallots, onions, and wine. Cover, reduce heat, and simmer for 30 minutes. Add mushrooms, cover, and simmer for 5 more minutes.

With a slotted spoon, remove chicken and vegetables (reserving sauce in pan) and arrange in a shallow 4-quart casserole or Dutch oven. Stir about ½ cup of the sauce into cornstarch and whisk until smooth. Return mixture to pan and cook, stirring, until sauce boils and thickens.

Sprinkle bacon over chicken and spoon sauce over all. (At this point you may cool, cover, and refrigerate until next day.)

Bake, covered, in a 350° oven for about 25 minutes (35 to 40 minutes, if refrigerated) or until sauce is bubbly and meat near bone is no longer pink when slashed. Makes 6 to 8 servings.

Chicken & Dumplings

Years ago, a meal of chicken and dumplings was the family's favorite Sunday dinner. Our updated version calls for adding poppy seeds to the dumplings and using chicken legs with thighs attached instead of the classic stewing hen. You can bake the chicken in the oven or on the stovetop.

    4 tablespoons butter or margarine
    6 whole chicken legs with thighs
          attached (about 3 lbs. *total*)
    1 large onion, finely chopped
    4 tablespoons all-purpose flour
    1⅔ cups chicken broth
    ⅓ cup dry white wine
    ½ teaspoon salt
    ¼ teaspoon pepper
    2 cups milk
       Dumplings (recipe follows)

In a 5-quart Dutch oven or heat-resistant casserole over medium heat, melt butter. Add chicken, a few pieces at a time, and cook until well browned on all sides. Remove and set aside.

To pan drippings, add onion and cook until soft. Blend in flour and cook, stirring, until bubbly. Gradually pour in broth and wine and continue cooking and stirring until sauce boils and thickens. Add salt, pepper, milk, and chicken.

Bake, covered, in a 375° oven (or cover and simmer over low heat) for 50 minutes. Skim off and discard fat.

Mix dumpling batter and drop onto hot chicken in 6 mounds. Cook, uncovered, on stovetop

(Continued on page 19)

over medium heat for 10 minutes; then cover and cook for 10 more minutes or until dumplings are cooked through. Serve immediately. Makes 6 servings.

Dumplings. Mix 2 cups **baking mix (biscuit mix)** with 1 tablespoon **poppy seeds**; stir in ⅔ cup **milk** until evenly moistened.

Sesame Chicken in Tarragon Cream

Crunchy sesame seeds coat chicken pieces that bake in a wine broth for 30 minutes. Then you cover the chicken with tender-crisp pieces of celery, onions, and mushrooms floating in a rich, tarragon-flavored cream sauce. The entire dish returns to the oven for more baking, followed by a last-minute sprinkling of toasted sesame seeds.

- ⅓ cup *each* **all-purpose flour and sesame seeds**
- ¾ teaspoon **salt**
- ¼ teaspoon **pepper**
- 1 **broiler-fryer chicken (3 to 3½ lbs.), cut in pieces**
- ¼ cup **salad oil**
- ½ cup **dry white wine**
- 1 cup **chicken broth**
- 1 small **onion, coarsely chopped**
- 3 stalks **celery, thinly sliced**
- ¼ pound **mushrooms, thinly sliced**
- 1 tablespoon *each* **butter or margarine and all-purpose flour**
- ½ cup **sour cream or unflavored yogurt**
- ¾ teaspoon **dry tarragon**
  About 2 tablespoons **sesame seeds**

Nothing rivals the taste of slow-cooked, hearty beef stew with vegetables (page 4). Crusty three wheat bread (page 87) gets its unusual shape when baked in coffee can.

In a small bag, combine the ⅓ cup *each* flour and sesame seeds, along with salt and pepper. Place chicken, a few pieces at a time, in bag and shake to coat completely.

Heat oil in a wide frying pan over medium heat. Add chicken, a few pieces at a time, and cook until well browned on all sides. Transfer chicken (reserve pan juices) to a shallow 3-quart casserole or 9 by 13-inch baking dish. Pour in wine and ½ cup of the chicken broth. Bake, covered, in a 350° oven for 30 minutes.

Meanwhile, to pan juices, add onion, celery, and mushrooms. Cook over low heat for about 10 minutes.

Add butter and when it melts, blend in the 1 tablespoon flour; raise heat to medium and cook, stirring, until bubbly. Gradually pour in remaining ½ cup chicken broth and sour cream and continue cooking and stirring until sauce just begins to boil. Stir in tarragon and spoon sauce over chicken. Return casserole, uncovered, to oven for 20 more minutes or until thigh meat near bone is no longer pink when slashed.

Meanwhile, spread the 2 tablespoons sesame seeds in a pan and cook over low heat, shaking pan occasionally, until seeds turn golden (about 2 minutes). Sprinkle over chicken before serving. Makes 4 servings.

Baked Chicken Paprika

No special ingredients are needed for this easy chicken casserole. Four simple seasonings—paprika, sugar, salt, and pepper—are combined and sprinkled over chicken pieces, which then bake in the oven for about 45 minutes. A perfect accompaniment is the flavorful carrot and rice casserole (page 83) that can bake in the oven at the same time.

- 1 **broiler-fryer chicken (3 to 3½ lbs.), cut in pieces**
  Butter or margarine
- 1 teaspoon **paprika**
- ¾ teaspoon **salt**
- ½ teaspoon **sugar**
- ⅛ teaspoon **pepper**

Arrange chicken, skin side down, in a lightly buttered shallow 3-quart casserole or 9 by 13-inch baking dish. Mix together paprika, salt, sugar, and pepper; sprinkle over chicken.

Bake, uncovered, in a 400° oven for about 35 minutes. Turn pieces over and bake for 10 to 15 more minutes or until thigh meat near bone is no longer pink when slashed. Makes 4 servings.

Chicken with Potatoes & Carrots

Crumb-coated chicken quarters, flavored with cornmeal and a hint of curry, bake in a shallow casserole along with small whole carrots and potatoes. The result is a delicious meal-in-one entrée suitable for company.

- ¼ cup *each* **fine dry bread crumbs and cornmeal**
- 1½ teaspoons **curry powder**
- ¾ teaspoon **salt**
- ⅛ teaspoon **pepper**
- 1 **broiler-fryer chicken (3 to 3½ lbs.), cut into quarters**
- ½ cup **butter or margarine**
- 8 small **carrots, peeled**
- 8 small **thin-skinned potatoes (about 1½ inches in diameter)**
  Chopped parsley

In a small bag, combine crumbs, cornmeal, curry powder, salt, and pepper. Place chicken quarters, one at a time, in bag and shake to coat completely; set aside.

Add butter to a shallow 3-quart casserole or 9 by 13-inch baking dish; set in oven while it preheats to 400°. As soon as butter is melted, remove casserole from oven. Carefully tilt pan slightly so butter collects in one corner. Roll carrots and potatoes in butter to coat evenly, then push vegetables aside and coat chicken with butter in the same manner. Arrange quarters, skin side down, beside vegetables.

Bake, uncovered, in a 400° oven for 30 minutes. Turn vegetables and chicken quarters over and bake for about 20 to 25 more minutes or until vegetables are tender when pierced and meat near bone is no longer pink when slashed. Garnish with parsley. Makes 4 servings.

Spiced Chicken & Peaches

Chicken pieces nestle in a delicately spiced orange sauce. Fresh peach slices added at the last minute help to counteract the tanginess of the sauce.

- 1 broiler-fryer chicken (3 to 3½ lbs.), cut in pieces
- 2 cups orange juice
- 1 teaspoon *each* salt and ground ginger
- ½ teaspoon ground nutmeg
- 1 clove garlic, minced or pressed
- 2 tablespoons all-purpose flour blended with 2 tablespoons water
- 2 tablespoons grated orange peel
- ¼ teaspoon salt
  Dash of pepper
- 2 large peaches

Arrange chicken, skin side up, in a shallow 3-quart casserole or 9 by 13-inch baking dish. Pour orange juice over chicken. In a cup, combine the 1 teaspoon salt with ginger, nutmeg, and garlic; sprinkle over chicken.

Bake, uncovered, in a 350° oven for 50 minutes or until thigh meat near bone is no longer pink when slashed.

Drain cooking liquid from casserole and measure; you should have 1½ cups. If not, add water to make 1½ cups or boil until reduced to 1½ cups. Stir in flour mixture and cook, stirring, until sauce boils and thickens. Add orange peel, the ¼ teaspoon salt, and pepper.

Peel, pit, and slice peaches; arrange on top of chicken pieces and spoon sauce over all. Return to oven for 5 more minutes or until heated through. Makes 4 servings.

Oven-sautéed Garlic Chicken

Here's one of the easiest methods for preparing oven-baked chicken. All the ingredients go together very quickly and you use only one pan.

- 4 tablespoons butter or margarine
- 1 large onion, thinly sliced and separated into rings
- 6 to 8 pieces (breasts, legs, and thighs) broiler-fryer chicken (about 2 lbs. *total*)
- 2 teaspoons paprika
- 1 teaspoon salt
- ¼ cup *each* catsup and dry white wine
- 6 cloves garlic, peeled

Place butter in a shallow 3-quart casserole or 9 by 13-inch baking dish; set in oven while it preheats to 350°. Scatter onion rings over bottom of casserole. With a brush, baste a little melted butter over chicken pieces and arrange them

over onions. Sprinkle chicken with paprika and salt.

Blend catsup and wine; carefully pour into casserole (but not directly over chicken pieces). Tuck in whole garlic cloves.

Bake, covered, in a 350° oven for about 45 minutes. Uncover and bake for 15 more minutes or until thigh meat near bone is no longer pink when slashed. Discard garlic and serve chicken with pan juices. Makes 4 to 6 servings.

Mexican Baked Chicken

In this quickly assembled, flavorful casserole, chicken pieces simmer in a thick tomato sauce laced with green chiles and ripe olives. Cheddar cheese, added 10 minutes before serving time, melts into a golden brown topping.

- 8 pieces (breasts, legs, and thighs) broiler-fryer chicken (about 3 lbs. *total*)
  About ⅓ cup all-purpose flour
- 2 or 3 tablespoons salad oil
- 1 can (15 oz.) tomato sauce
- ½ cup water
- 2 crushed chicken bouillon cubes
- 1 can (4 oz.) diced green chiles, drained
- 1 can (4 oz.) chopped ripe olives, drained
- 2 tablespoons wine vinegar
- ¾ teaspoon *each* ground cumin and garlic salt
- 2 tablespoons instant minced onion
- 2 cups (8 oz.) shredded Cheddar cheese

Coat chicken pieces with flour; shake off excess. Heat oil in a wide frying pan over medium heat. Add chicken, a few pieces at a time, and cook until well browned on all sides. Arrange pieces in a shallow 3-quart casserole or 9 by 13-inch baking dish.

Discard oil in frying pan and wipe clean. Add tomato sauce, water, bouillon cubes, chiles, olives, vinegar, cumin, garlic salt, and onion. Bring to a boil. Reduce heat and simmer, uncovered, until sauce thickens slightly (about 3 minutes). Spoon sauce over chicken. (At this point you may cool, cover, and refrigerate until next day.)

Bake, covered, in a 350° oven for about 50 minutes (60 to 70 minutes, if refrigerated) or until thigh meat near bone is no longer pink when slashed. Remove cover, skim off and discard fat, and sprinkle with cheese. Return to oven, uncovered, for about 10 more minutes or until cheese is melted. Makes 4 to 6 servings.

Chilean Corn & Chicken Pie

In Chile, where so much cooking is done with corn, one of the most popular dishes is *pastel de choclo*, a meaty chicken pie topped with ground corn instead of pastry. Just before baking, the corn topping receives a sprinkling of sugar that melts into a thin golden skin.

- 3 tablespoons butter or margarine
- 1 medium-size onion, chopped
- 1 clove garlic, minced or pressed
- 2 tablespoons all-purpose flour
- 1 chicken bouillon cube dissolved in 1 cup boiling water
- ½ teaspoon *each* paprika and ground cumin
- ¼ teaspoon crushed red pepper (cayenne)
- 3 cups cooked chicken, torn into bite-size pieces
- 2 hard-cooked eggs, chopped
- ½ cup pitted ripe olives
- ¼ cup raisins
- 1 can (1 lb.) cream-style corn
- 1 egg, beaten
- 4 to 8 teaspoons sugar

In a wide frying pan over medium heat, melt 2 tablespoons of the butter. Add onion and garlic and cook until onion is soft. Blend in 1 tablespoon of the flour and cook, stirring, until bubbly. Gradually pour in bouillon and continue cooking and stirring until sauce

boils and thickens. Stir in paprika, cumin, and red pepper.

Remove from heat and add chicken, hard-cooked eggs, olives, and raisins. Spoon mixture into 4 lightly greased individual ramekins (1½-cup size) or a lightly greased shallow 1½-quart casserole or 9-inch-square baking dish.

Wipe frying pan clean. Over medium heat, melt remaining 1 tablespoon butter. Blend in remaining 1 tablespoon flour and the corn; cook, stirring, until bubbly. Remove from heat. Add egg; stir until well blended.

Spoon corn sauce evenly over chicken mixture in each ramekin, then sprinkle each top with 1 to 2 teaspoons sugar. (If using a casserole, generously sprinkle with 4 to 8 teaspoons sugar.)

Bake ramekins, uncovered, in a 350° oven for 25 minutes (35 minutes for casserole). Then broil about 2 inches from heat for 3 to 5 minutes or until top is golden brown. Makes 4 servings.

Turkey & Tortilla Casserole

Devising something different to use up leftover turkey can be challenging. But this out-of-the-ordinary casserole features diced turkey, ripe olives, two kinds of cheese, and corn tortillas.

- 4 to 5 cups diced cooked turkey or chicken
- 1 can (10¾ oz.) condensed cream of mushroom soup
- 1 can (4 oz.) diced green chiles, drained
- 1 can (7 oz.) green chili salsa
- 1 can (2¼ oz.) sliced ripe olives, drained
- ⅓ cup thinly sliced green onions (including tops)
- ¾ teaspoon ground cumin
- 8 corn tortillas, cut in ½-inch strips
- 2 cups (8 oz.) *each* shredded jack and Cheddar cheese

In a bowl, combine turkey, soup, chiles, salsa, olives, onion, and cumin; set aside. Arrange half the tortilla strips in a well-greased shallow 3-quart casserole or 9 by 13-inch baking dish. Cover evenly with half the turkey mixture and all the jack cheese. Top with remaining tortilla strips and remaining turkey. Sprinkle Cheddar cheese evenly over all. (At this point you may cover and refrigerate until next day.)

Bake, uncovered, in a 350° oven for 30 minutes or until cheese is melted and mixture is heated through. (If refrigerated, bake, covered, for 30 minutes; uncover and bake for 15 more minutes.) Let stand for about 5 minutes before cutting into squares. Makes 6 to 8 servings.

Florentine Turkey Rolls

Sliced turkey breast, pounded into thin steaks and wrapped around a savory filling of spinach, mushrooms, and cheese, makes an inexpensive and tempting substitute for veal. To slice the turkey breast more easily, partially freeze it for about 1½ hours before slicing. Complete the menu with steamed asparagus or broccoli and a green salad.

- 5 tablespoons butter or margarine
- ½ pound mushrooms, thinly sliced
- ¼ cup all-purpose flour
- ¼ teaspoon *each* ground nutmeg and white pepper
- 1 chicken bouillon cube dissolved in ¾ cup boiling water
- ¾ cup *each* dry white wine and half-and-half (light cream)
- 2½ pounds turkey breast
- 1 package (10 oz.) frozen chopped spinach, thawed and drained well
- 1½ cups (6 oz.) shredded Swiss or jack cheese

(Continued on next page)

In a wide frying pan over medium heat, melt butter. Add mushrooms and cook, stirring, until soft. Blend in flour, nutmeg, and pepper and cook, stirring, until bubbly. Gradually pour in bouillon, wine, and half-and-half and continue cooking and stirring until sauce boils and thickens; set aside.

Remove skin and bone from turkey breast. Place, cavity side down, on a board. With a sharp knife, cut breast lengthwise (with the grain) into 6 long thin steaks. Place each steak between 2 sheets of plastic film on a cutting board. With a mallet, pound breasts until each is about ¼ inch thick. Repeat for remaining turkey steaks.

Mix together spinach, 1 cup of the cheese, and 3 tablespoons of the mushroom sauce. Place ¼ cup of the mixture at one end of each pounded turkey steak; tucking in sides, roll up tightly into a bundle.

Place bundles, seam side down, in a lightly greased shallow 2-quart casserole or 9-inch-square baking dish. Spoon remaining mushroom sauce over turkey. (At this point, you may cool, cover and refrigerate until next day.)

Bake, covered, in a 400° oven for 45 minutes (55 minutes, if refrigerated); uncover and sprinkle with remaining ½ cup cheese. Bake, uncovered, for 5 more minutes or until cheese is melted and mixture is heated through. Makes 6 servings.

Turkey Steak Parmesan

Here is an innovative recipe for uncooked turkey breast that is sliced and pounded into thin steaks. They are coated with a bread crumb and cheese mixture, with mozzarella cheese. Crusty rolls and a crisp green salad would complete the meal.

2 to 2½-pound turkey breast
⅓ cup *each* grated Parmesan cheese and fine dry bread crumbs
1½ teaspoons salt
¼ teaspoon pepper
¼ cup all-purpose flour
1 egg beaten with 1 tablespoon water
¼ cup salad oil
2 tablespoons butter or margarine
1 medium-size onion, finely chopped
1 clove garlic, minced or pressed
1 can (6 oz.) tomato paste
1½ cups hot water
½ teaspoon *each* sugar and oregano leaves
1 teaspoon dry basil
½ pound mozzarella or jack cheese, thinly sliced

Remove skin and bone from turkey breast. Place, cavity side down, on a board. With a sharp knife, cut breast lengthwise (with the grain) into 6 long thin steaks. Place each steak between 2 sheets of plastic wrap on a cutting board. With a mallet, pound breast until each is about ¼ inch thick. Repeat for remaining turkey steaks.

Combine Parmesan cheese and bread crumbs; set aside. Sprinkle steaks evenly with ½ teaspoon of the salt and a little of the pepper. Coat with flour; shake off excess. Dip each steak in egg mixture and coat with bread crumb mixture.

Heat oil in a wide frying pan over medium-high heat. Add turkey steaks and cook quickly until just browned. Remove from pan (reserve pan juices) and arrange in a single layer in a shallow 3-quart casserole or 9 by 13-inch baking dish.

To pan juices, add butter and melt. Add onion and cook until soft. Stir in garlic, tomato paste, hot water, sugar, oregano, basil, and remaining 1 teaspoon salt. Scrape brown particles free from pan. Reduce heat and simmer, uncovered, for about 5 minutes.

Spoon about three-quarters of the sauce over steaks, top with mozzarella cheese and remaining sauce. (At this point you may cool, cover, and refrigerate until next day.)

Bake, uncovered, in a 350° oven for 30 minutes (45 minutes, if refrigerated) or until bubbly and lightly browned. Makes 6 servings.

Fish & Celery Root Ramekins

Oven-poached fish fillets—either lingcod or sea bass—and shredded celery root bake in individual ramekins, then are covered with a rich, herb-flavored shrimp sauce. This unusual seafood combination is perfect for a company entrée served with a lightly seasoned rice dish and a green vegetable.

2 tablespoons lemon juice
About 1 cup chicken broth or dry white wine
1 small onion, chopped
1 celery root (about ¾ lb.), peeled and shredded
4 lingcod or sea bass fillets (6 to 8 oz. *each*), cut 1 inch thick
2 tablespoons *each* butter or margarine and all-purpose flour
¼ cup whipping cream
¾ teaspoon thyme leaves
½ pound small cooked shrimp
Salt and ground white pepper

Mix lemon juice, 1 cup of the broth, onion, and celery root. Divide mixture among 4 individual ramekins (about 2-cup size). Place a fish fillet in each ramekin.

Bake, covered tightly, in a 400° oven for 20 to 25 minutes or until fish flakes readily when prodded in thickest portion with a fork.

(Continued on page 24)

Lattice-style crust covers delicious filling of tender chicken and sautéed vegetables in lemon cream sauce. Recipe is on page 12.

Holding fish in place with a wide spatula, drain and reserve juices. Keep fish warm. Boil juices to reduce to 1 cup or add more broth to make 1 cup.

In a pan over medium heat, melt butter. Blend in flour and cook, stirring, until bubbly. Gradually stir in reserved fish juices, cream, and thyme and continue cooking and stirring until sauce boils and thickens. Add shrimp and season to taste with salt and pepper. Spoon sauce over fish. Makes 4 servings.

Savory Fish Bake

Tender sole fillets, garnished with thin onion slices and shredded carrot, bake in a simple sauce. You can use either fresh sole or frozen fillets without first thawing them.

- 2 **pounds fresh or frozen sole fillets**
  Butter or margarine
- 1 **small onion, thinly sliced**
- ¾ **cup shredded carrot**
- 1 **can (10¾ oz.) condensed cream of celery soup**
- 2 **tablespoons dry white wine or milk**
- 1 **tablespoon lemon juice**
- ½ **teaspoon marjoram leaves or thyme leaves**
- ¼ **teaspoon garlic powder**
- ¼ **cup grated Parmesan cheese**
  Ground nutmeg

Arrange fresh fish (overlap thin edges) in a buttered shallow 3-quart casserole or 9 by 13-inch baking dish. Or arrange blocks of frozen fish (do not thaw) slightly apart in a shallow 2-quart casserole or 9-inch-square baking dish. Top with onion slices and sprinkle evenly with shredded carrot.

In a bowl, combine soup, wine, lemon juice, marjoram, and garlic powder. Spoon mixture over fish and sprinkle with Parmesan cheese. Dust lightly with nutmeg.

Bake, uncovered, in a 450° oven for 15 to 20 minutes for fresh fish, 40 to 50 minutes for frozen, or until fish flakes readily when prodded in thickest portion with a fork. Makes 4 to 6 servings.

Quick Sole & Shrimp Casserole

Sole fillets—either fresh or frozen —are layered with shrimp and mushrooms and baked in this quick seafood casserole. What could be simpler and more tempting?

- **Butter or margarine**
- 1 **pound fresh or frozen sole fillets (thawed, if frozen)**
- ¼ **pound small cooked shrimp**
- 3 **tablespoons fine dry bread crumbs**
- ¼ **teaspoon pepper**
- 2 **tablespoons lemon juice**
- ¼ **pound mushrooms, thinly sliced**
- 2 **tablespoons tartar sauce or mayonnaise**
- 2 **tablespoons thinly sliced green onion (including top)**
- 1 **clove garlic, minced or pressed**
- 1½ **tablespoons butter or margarine, softened**
- ¼ **cup dry vermouth (optional)**

Generously butter a shallow 1½-quart casserole or 9-inch-square baking dish. Place half the fish fillets in an even layer in pan. Sprinkle evenly with half the shrimp, bread crumbs, pepper,

lemon juice, and sliced mushrooms. Repeat layers. Combine tartar sauce, green onion, garlic, and softened butter; dot over mushrooms. Drizzle evenly with vermouth, if desired.

Bake, covered, in a 350° oven for 30 minutes or until fish flakes readily when prodded in thickest portion with a fork. Makes 4 servings.

Sole in Wine Sauce

There's no chance that the fish in this casserole will be dry or overcooked; the herb and wine-flavored sauce keeps it moist during baking. We used sole fillets but you may want to substitute any thin, mild fish fillets.

- 2 **pounds fresh or frozen sole fillets (thawed, if frozen)**
- 2 **tablespoons *each* lemon juice and dry white wine**
  Dash of salt and pepper
- 4 **tablespoons butter or margarine**
- 4 **tablespoons all-purpose flour**
- 2 **cups milk**
- ¼ **teaspoon pepper**
- ¾ **teaspoon dry mustard**
- 1 **teaspoon Worcestershire**
- ½ **teaspoon dry tarragon**
- 2 **tablespoons *each* chopped parsley, green onion (including top), and grated Parmesan cheese**
- ¼ **cup dry sherry**

Sprinkle fillets with lemon juice, wine, and salt and pepper; refrigerate for several hours.

In a 2-quart pan over medium heat, melt butter. Blend in flour and cook, stirring, until bubbly. Gradually pour in milk and continue cooking and stirring until sauce boils and thickens. Add the ¼ teaspoon pepper, along with mustard, Worcestershire, tarragon, parsley, green onion, cheese, and sherry. Reduce heat and simmer, stirring occasionally, for 5 minutes.

Arrange fillets, (overlap thin edges) in a single layer in a lightly greased shallow 3-quart casserole or 9 by 13-inch baking dish. Spoon sauce over fish.

Bake, uncovered, in a 350° oven for about 30 minutes or until fish flakes readily when prodded in thickest portion with a fork. Makes about 4 to 6 servings.

Polynesian Shrimp & Rice

This Haitian seafood casserole combines shrimp, rice, tomatoes, lima beans, and chopped bacon in an unusual blend of flavors. Accompany this entrée with a crusty bread, green salad, and a bottle of dry white wine.

1 to 1½ pounds medium-size raw shrimp, shelled and deveined
3 strips bacon, cut in ½-inch pieces
1 large onion, chopped
2 tablespoons salad oil
2 cups white rice
1 package (10 oz.) frozen Fordhook limas
2 large tomatoes, cut in wedges
6 tablespoons chopped parsley
1½ teaspoons *each* salt and vinegar
½ teaspoon liquid hot pepper seasoning (optional)
¼ teaspoon pepper
4 cups boiling water
2 to 3 tablespoons butter or margarine
Lime wedges

In a 5-quart pan over medium heat, cook bacon until limp. Stir in onion and cook until soft. Add salad oil and shrimp and cook, stirring, until shrimp turn pink.

Mix in rice and stir to coat with oil. Add limas, tomatoes, 4 tablespoons of the parsley, salt, vinegar, hot pepper seasoning (if desired), pepper, and boiling water. Bring mixture to a boil. Cover, reduce heat, and simmer for about 20 minutes or until rice has absorbed all the liquid.

Mix in butter, then spoon mixture into a serving dish. Garnish with remaining parsley. Pass lime wedges. Makes about 6 servings.

Extraordinary Tuna & Noodle Casserole

No longer will tuna and noodles be the unimaginative dish you serve your family when all else fails. This delicious variation is full of fresh tastes. Celery seeds and dill perk up the flavor; a little sherry adds a touch of class; and fancy-shaped pasta instead of the usual flat noodle gives the dish a whole new look.

6 ounces medium-size, fancy-shaped pasta (shells, egg twists, bows, wheels, etc.)
Boiling salted water
Butter or margarine
2 cans (about 7 oz. *each*) chunk-style tuna, drained and flaked
1 package (10 oz.) frozen peas, thawed
½ pound mushrooms, sliced and sautéed (optional)
½ teaspoon garlic salt
¼ teaspoon *each* dill weed and celery seeds
⅛ teaspoon pepper
2 cans (10¾ oz. *each*) condensed cream of mushroom soup
¼ cup milk
3 tablespoons dry sherry
3 slices bread
2 tablespoons melted butter or margarine

Cook noodles in boiling salted water according to package directions; drain well.

Lightly butter a shallow 2½-quart casserole or 7 by 11-inch baking dish and arrange half the tuna in the bottom. Combine peas, mushrooms (if desired), garlic salt, dill weed, celery seeds, and pepper. Spread half the mixture over tuna.

Mix together soup, milk, and sherry; spoon half the soup mix-

ture into casserole and top with all the noodles. Repeat layering, ending with soup mixture. Tear bread into coarse crumbs; you should have ½ cup. Combine bread crumbs and melted butter; sprinkle over top. (At this point you may cover and refrigerate until next day.)

Bake, uncovered, in a 350° oven for about 30 minutes (40 minutes, if refrigerated) or until top is bubbly and lightly browned. Makes about 6 servings.

Tuna Spaghetti Pie

Canned tuna, cottage cheese, spinach, and Swiss cheese team up in a delicious filling for this unusual pie. But what's really different is the crust—it is made with cooked spaghetti, Parmesan cheese, and eggs. You can use any shallow 1½-quart casserole or 9-inch pie pan.

6 ounces spaghetti
Boiling salted water
2 tablespoons butter or margarine
⅓ cup grated Parmesan cheese
2 eggs, well beaten
Butter or margarine
1 package (10 oz.) frozen chopped spinach, thawed and well drained
2 cans (about 7 oz. *each*) chunk-style tuna, drained and flaked
1 medium-size onion, chopped
1 cup small curd cream-style cottage cheese
1 tablespoon Dijon mustard
½ teaspoon *each* dill weed and garlic salt
1 cup (4 oz.) shredded Swiss cheese

Cook spaghetti in boiling salted water according to package directions; drain well. Combine spaghetti with the 2 tablespoons butter, Parmesan cheese, and eggs. Spread over bottom and sides of a well-buttered shallow 1½-quart casserole or 9-inch pie pan (1½ inches deep).

(Continued on page 27)

Stir together spinach, tuna, onion, cottage cheese, mustard, dill, garlic salt, and ½ cup of the Swiss cheese; blend well. Spread in spaghetti-lined dish. (At this point you may cover and refrigerate until next day.)

Bake, uncovered, in a 350° oven for 30 minutes (45 minutes, if refrigerated) or until set. Sprinkle with remaining Swiss cheese and return to oven for 5 more minutes or until cheese is melted. Makes about 6 servings.

Seafood-stuffed Pasta Shells

(Pictured on facing page)

These elegant, shrimp-filled tubes of pasta (manicotti) are crowned with a fontina cheese sauce flavored ever so slightly with nutmeg, white pepper, and vermouth. The pasta simmers in a zesty tomato sauce laced with chopped vegetables and herbs.

- 2 tablespoons butter or margarine
- 1 medium-size onion, finely chopped
- 1 medium-size carrot, shredded
- ¼ cup chopped parsley
- 1 can (1 lb.) tomatoes
- 1 cup chicken broth
- 1 teaspoon dry basil
- ¾ pound cooked fresh or canned crab, flaked
- ½ pound small cooked shrimp
- 3 green onions (including tops), thinly sliced
- 1 cup (4 oz.) shredded fontina cheese
- 8 large manicotti or other tube-shaped pasta
  Boiling salted water
  Fontina white sauce (recipe follows)
- ½ cup grated Parmesan cheese

Tempting seafood-stuffed pasta shells are simmered in vegetable-laced tomato sauce, then topped with delicate fontina cheese sauce and grated Parmesan. Recipe is on this page.

In a wide frying pan over medium heat, melt butter. Add onion and carrot and cook until soft. Stir in parsley, tomatoes (break up with a spoon) and their liquid, broth, and basil. Reduce heat and simmer, uncovered, for about 30 minutes or until sauce thickens. Set aside.

Combine crab, shrimp, green onions, and fontina cheese; set filling aside.

Cook manicotti in boiling salted water according to package directions just until *al dente* (still slightly firm); *do not overcook.* Rinse with cold water and drain well. Meanwhile, prepare fontina white sauce.

To assemble casserole, stuff each manicotti with about 4 tablespoons of the filling. Spoon half the tomato sauce into a shallow 3-quart casserole or 9 by 13-inch baking dish. Arrange filled pasta side by side in sauce. Pour some of the remaining sauce into casserole (but not directly over pasta). Spoon white sauce down the center of the manicotti and sprinkle with ⅓ cup of the Parmesan. (At this point you may cool, cover, and refrigerate until next day.)

Bake, uncovered, in a 375° oven for 20 to 25 minutes (35 minutes, if refrigerated) or until lightly browned and heated through. Sprinkle with remaining cheese and offer any remaining sauce. Makes 4 or 6 servings.

Fontina white sauce. In a wide frying pan over medium heat, melt ¼ cup **butter** or margarine. Add 1 small **onion** (finely chopped) and cook until soft. Blend in 2 tablespoons all-purpose **flour** and cook, stirring, until bubbly. Gradually pour in ¾ cup *each* **milk** and **chicken broth** and continue cooking and stirring until sauce boils and thickens. Remove from heat and add 1 cup (about 4 oz.) shredded **fontina cheese,** 2 tablespoons **dry vermouth,** and ⅛ teaspoon *each* **ground nutmeg** and **white pepper.** Stir just until cheese melts.

Baked Cod with Capers

Packages of bright orange-red kippered cod or kippered salmon can be found in almost any market. In this recipe, an aromatic white sauce covers layers of flaked fish, onions, and potatoes.

- 3 medium-size potatoes (about 1 lb. total), peeled and sliced
  Boiling salted water
- 4 tablespoons butter or margarine
- 2 medium-size onions, thinly sliced
- ½ to ¾ pound kippered cod or salmon
- 2 tablespoons all-purpose flour
- 1¼ cups milk
- 1 teaspoon *each* paprika and Dijon mustard
- ½ teaspoon salt
- ⅛ teaspoon pepper
- 2 tablespoons *each* drained chopped capers and lemon juice
  Chopped parsley (optional)

Cook potatoes in boiling salted water just until tender when pierced (about 5 minutes). Drain well and arrange in a shallow 2-quart casserole or 9-inch-square baking dish.

In a wide frying pan over medium heat, melt 2 tablespoons of the butter. Add onions and cook until soft; spoon evenly over potatoes. Flake fish with a fork, discarding dark skin and bones; distribute fish evenly over onions.

In frying pan, melt remaining 2 tablespoons butter. Blend in flour and cook, stirring, until bubbly. Gradually pour in milk and continue cooking and stirring until sauce boils and thickens. Season with paprika, mustard, salt, pepper, capers, and lemon juice. Spoon sauce over fish. (At this point you may cool, cover, and refrigerate until next day.)

Bake, uncovered, in a 350° oven for 20 to 25 minutes (30 to 35 minutes, if refrigerated) or until heated through. Garnish with parsley, if desired. Makes about 4 servings.

Here are casseroles to please a crowd— & they're portable

Veal Scaloppine with Teleme

(Pictured on front cover)

Thin slices (*scaloppa,* in Italian) of succulent, boneless veal are dipped in egg and coated with bread crumbs. Then they're quickly sautéed, layered with teleme cheese, and baked in a rich tomato sauce. At the last minute, pesto sauce is added, along with cherry tomatoes and a sprig of fresh basil for garnish.

Assembling this impressive dish takes time, so you may want to prepare it a day in advance. Our recipe serves 10 to 12, but it can easily be cut in half for a special family meal.

      Tomato sauce (recipe follows)
  3   eggs
  ⅓   cup water
      About 1½ cups fine dry bread crumbs
  ½   teaspoon oregano leaves
  3½ to 4 pounds boneless veal, trimmed and pounded for scaloppine
  8   tablespoons (¼ lb.) butter or margarine, or a combination of half butter or margarine and half salad oil (about 4 tablespoons each)
      Salt and pepper
  ½ to ¾ pound teleme cheese or mozzarella, thinly sliced
  ½   cup grated Parmesan cheese
      Pesto sauce (recipe follows)
      Sliced cherry tomatoes
      Basil or parsley sprig

Prepare tomato sauce as directed; set aside.

In a shallow dish, beat eggs with water. In another shallow dish, combine bread crumbs and oregano. Dip each slice of veal in egg, then coat both sides with bread crumb-oregano mixture. Lay pieces side by side until all are coated.

To cook veal, use 2 tablespoons butter or a butter-oil combination for each pound of veal. (Butter or margarine adds flavor and enhances browning but burns easily; a combination of butter and oil is flavorful and doesn't burn as readily.) Place a wide frying pan over medium-high heat. When pan is hot, coat surface with about 1 tablespoon butter or butter-oil combination; then add veal without crowding pieces. Add more butter, a teaspoon at a time, when pan appears dry.

Cook veal, turning once, until lightly browned (3 to 4 minutes *total*). Transfer browned veal to a rack or platter to cool slightly; sprinkle with salt and pepper.

Cover the bottom of a shallow 3½ or 4-quart casserole or baking dish with tomato sauce. Arrange veal in overlapping slices over sauce. Carefully tuck a slice of cheese in between overlapping veal.

Spoon tomato sauce into casserole, but not directly over veal; reserve any remaining sauce. Sprinkle veal and cheese with ¼ cup of the Parmesan cheese. (At this point you may cover and refrigerate until next day.)

Bake, uncovered, in a 350° oven for 20 to 25 minutes or until cheese begins to brown and casserole is heated through. (If refrigerated, bake, covered, for 30 minutes; then uncover and bake for 15 to 20 more minutes.)

While casserole bakes, prepare pesto sauce. Spoon pesto sauce down center of dish; garnish with tomato slices and basil sprig. Serve with remaining tomato sauce, if any, and remaining ¼ cup Parmesan cheese. Makes 10 to 12 servings.

Tomato sauce. In a wide frying pan over medium heat, melt 4 tablespoons **butter** or margarine. Add

2 **onions,** finely chopped, and 1 large **carrot,** shredded; cook until onions are soft. Stir in ½ cup chopped **parsley,** 2 cans (1 lb. *each*) **tomatoes** (break up with a spoon) and their liquid, 1 can (16 oz.) **tomato sauce,** 2 cups **chicken broth,** and 2 teaspoons **dry basil.** Bring to a boil. Cover, reduce heat, and simmer for 15 minutes. Uncover and continue cooking, stirring occasionally, until sauce is thickened (about 30 minutes).

Pesto sauce. Wash and thoroughly dry 2 cups lightly packed fresh **basil leaves.** Place in a blender or food processor along with 1 cup **grated Parmesan cheese** and ½ cup **olive oil.** Whirl until basil is finely chopped. Use at once, or place in a small jar and cover with a thin layer of olive oil to keep pesto from darkening. Refrigerate for up to 1 week. Makes about 1 cup.

Chicken & Barley Casserole

Boneless chicken breasts, sliced mushrooms, and tiny pearl barley combine in this tempting casserole. The finishing touch is a last-minute ingredient—delicate artichoke hearts.

> 6 whole chicken breasts (about 1 lb. *each*), split, skinned, and boned
>   Salt, pepper, and paprika
> 6 tablespoons butter or margarine
> ¾ pound mushrooms, sliced
> 1½ cups pearl barley
> 2 medium-size onions, chopped
> 1½ teaspoons dry basil
> 3 cans (14 oz. *each*) chicken broth
> ⅓ cup dry sherry
> 2 packages (about 9 oz. *each*) frozen artichoke hearts, thawed
>   Chopped parsley

Sprinkle chicken thoroughly with salt, pepper, and paprika. In a wide frying pan over medium heat, melt 2 tablespoons of the butter. Add chicken breasts, a few pieces at a time, and cook until well browned on both sides. Add up to 2 more tablespoons of the butter, as needed. Remove chicken from pan and set aside.

In same pan, melt remaining 2 tablespoons butter. Add mushrooms and cook until soft. Remove mushrooms from pan and set aside. To the pan juices, add barley and onions. Cook, stirring, until onions are soft. Add basil and 1½ cans of the broth. Cover, reduce heat, and simmer, stirring occasionally, for about 40 minutes.

Stir in mushrooms (reserve a few for garnish). Divide mixture between 2 large shallow casseroles and arrange chicken breasts on top. Combine remaining 1½ cans broth with sherry and carefully pour half over each casserole.

Bake, covered, in a 375° oven for 25 to 30 minutes or until barley is tender. During the last 10 minutes, gently mix in artichoke hearts.

To serve, skim off and discard fat, if any. Sprinkle with parsley and garnish with reserved mushrooms. Makes 8 to 12 servings.

Garlic Lamb Meatballs with Lemon Sauce

For a delightful change from traditional spaghetti and meatballs, you may want to try this version at your next buffet. The meatballs are made with ground lamb, chopped parsley, rosemary, and garlic; they rest on a bed of spaghetti that's flavored with a tangy lemon sauce.

> 3 pounds lean ground lamb
> 3 eggs, lightly beaten
> 10 to 15 cloves garlic, minced or pressed
> ¾ teaspoon dry rosemary
> 1½ teaspoons salt
> ½ teaspoon pepper
> 1½ cups finely chopped parsley
>   All-purpose flour
>   About 6 tablespoons salad oil
> 3 cups chicken broth
> 1½ packages (24 oz.) spaghetti
>   Boiling salted water
> 6 egg yolks
> ⅓ cup lemon juice
> 3 tablespoons grated lemon peel
>   Ground nutmeg
>   Salt and pepper
>   Additional chopped parsley

In a large bowl, combine lamb, beaten eggs, half the garlic, rosemary, the 1½ teaspoons salt, the ¼ teaspoon pepper, and ¾ cup of the parsley. Mix well and shape into 36 meatballs; coat lightly with flour.

Heat 2 tablespoons of the oil in a wide frying pan over medium-high heat. Add meatballs, a few at a time, and cook, turning, until well browned on all sides; add more oil, as needed. Remove meatballs and keep warm.

Skim off and discard fat from pan drippings. Add broth and bring to a boil, scraping crusty particles free from pan. Remove from heat.

Cook spaghetti in boiling salted water according to package directions; drain, transfer to a large platter, and keep warm.

In a large bowl, combine egg yolks, lemon juice, lemon peel, remaining minced garlic, and remaining ¾ cup parsley. With a wire whisk, beat egg mixture constantly while slowly adding broth mixture. Return egg-broth mixture to pan and cook, stirring, over medium heat just until thickened (about 2 minutes). Season to taste with nutmeg, salt, and pepper.

Pour sauce over spaghetti and stir to mix. Arrange meatballs on top and garnish with chopped parsley. Makes 12 servings.

Crab & Onion Pie

(Pictured on page 31)

Light, buttery pastry forms the crust for this golden crab and onion pie.

Buttery pastry (recipe follows)
- 1 cup (4 oz.) shredded Swiss, Samsoe, or Gruyère cheese
- ¾ pound cooked or canned crab meat, flaked
- ½ cup finely chopped onion
- 2 tablespoons dry sherry
- 3 tablespoons finely chopped parsley
- Dash of ground red pepper (cayenne)
- ¼ teaspoon dry tarragon
- 4 eggs
- 1 cup half-and-half (light cream)
- Paprika

Prepare pastry crust as directed. When crust is cool, sprinkle ¾ cup of the cheese over bottom of crust.

Combine crab, onion, sherry, 2 tablespoons of the parsley, red pepper, and tarragon; spoon mixture evenly over cheese. Beat eggs with cream and pour over crab. Sprinkle with remaining ¼ cup cheese and 1 tablespoon parsley; dust lightly with paprika.

Bake, uncovered, in a 350° oven for 50 to 60 minutes or until center appears firm when gently shaken. Let stand for a few minutes to cool before cutting into wedges. Makes about 6 servings.

Buttery pastry. In a bowl, combine 1½ cups all-purpose **flour** and ¼ teaspoon **salt**. Add 6 tablespoons **butter** or margarine, cut into chunks; mix to coat with flour.

With a pastry blender or 2 knives, cut butter into flour until coarse particles are formed. Stir in 2 **egg yolks**, then 2 to 3 tablespoons **water,** a little at a time, until pastry holds together. Shape into a ball.

Roll pastry out on a floured board or pastry cloth into a circle about 12 inches in diameter. Fit pastry into a 10-inch quiche or pie pan; trim edge. Prick bottom and side all over with a fork. Bake in a 400° oven for 8 to 10 minutes or until pastry begins to brown. Let cool on a wire rack before filling.

Salmon Florentine

Meaty salmon fillets, resting on a bed of fresh spinach, are covered with a flavorful sauce accented with lemon, mustard, and cheese.

- 4 tablespoons butter or margarine
- 1 large onion, chopped
- 1½ to 2 pounds spinach
- 1½ cups water
- 1 tablespoon lemon juice
- Salt and pepper
- 2 pounds salmon fillets
- 2 tablespoons all-purpose flour
- 1 teaspoon Dijon mustard
- 2 tablespoons grated Parmesan cheese
- About 1 tablespoon grated lemon peel

In a wide frying pan over medium heat, melt 2 tablespoons of the butter. Add onion and cook until soft. Remove and discard tough spinach stems. Wash and coarsely shred spinach leaves; add to pan. Cover and cook just until wilted. Turn mixture into a shallow 2-quart casserole.

Pour water into frying pan and add lemon juice, dash of salt and pepper, and salmon. Cover, reduce heat, and simmer until fish flakes readily when prodded in thickest portion with a fork (about 10 minutes). Lift out fish and arrange on spinach. Reserve 1 cup of the poaching liquid; discard remaining liquid (if any).

In pan, melt remaining 2 tablespoons butter. Blend in flour and cook, stirring, until bubbly. Gradually pour in reserved 1 cup poaching liquid and continue cooking and stirring until sauce boils and thickens. Season with mustard, cheese, and salt and pepper to taste. Pour over fish.

Bake, uncovered, in a 350° oven for 20 minutes or until heated through. Garnish with lemon peel. Makes 4 to 6 servings.

Crab & Spaghetti Bake

Flaky fresh crab, hard-cooked eggs, Cheddar cheese, and spaghetti star in this attractive seafood casserole.

- 6 ounces spaghetti or vermicelli
- Boiling salted water
- 2 tablespoons butter or margarine
- 1 large onion, chopped
- 1 can (10¾ oz.) condensed cream of mushroom soup
- 1 cup half-and-half (light cream)
- 1 tablespoon *each* Worcestershire and Dijon mustard
- ½ pound cooked fresh or canned crab
- 2 hard-cooked eggs, diced
- ½ cup thinly sliced water chestnuts
- 1 jar (2 oz.) sliced pimentos, drained
- Salt and ground red pepper (cayenne)
- ⅔ cup shredded sharp Cheddar cheese

Cook spaghetti in boiling salted water according to package directions; drain well.

In a 3-quart pan over medium heat, melt butter. Add onion and cook until soft. Blend in soup, half-and-half, Worcestershire, and mustard. Add spaghetti, crab, eggs, water chestnuts, and pimentos; toss gently. Season to taste with salt and red pepper.

Spoon spaghetti mixture into a lightly greased shallow 2-quart casserole or 9-inch-square baking dish. Sprinkle with cheese.

Bake, uncovered, in a 375° oven for about 25 minutes or until bubbly and heated through. Makes 6 servings.

Feast your eyes on this array of main-dish casseroles including (clockwise from top right) fila chicken and artichoke casserole (page 11), extra-spicy macaroni & cheese (page 37), savory fish stew with tomatoes (page 78), steak & kidney pie (page 52), beef stew (page 73), Swiss chard pie (page 40), ham & vegetable crêpes (page 57), delicate crab & onion pie (page 30), and lasagne (page 51).

MEATLESS ENTRÉES

Starring cheese, eggs & vegetables

Eggplant Enchiladas

Green chiles accent these eggplant-filled tortillas topped with canned enchilada sauce and shredded Cheddar cheese. Offer garnishes of guacamole, sliced ripe olives, chopped tomatoes, and sour cream.

- 4 tablespoons butter or margarine
- 1 large eggplant (about 1½ lbs.), cut into ½-inch cubes
- 2 cloves garlic, minced or pressed
- 1 medium-size onion, coarsely chopped
- 1 large green pepper, seeded and coarsely chopped
- 1 can (4 oz.) diced green chiles, drained
- 2½ cups (about 10 oz.) shredded Cheddar cheese
  Salt and pepper
- 2 cans (10 oz. *each*) enchilada sauce
- 12 corn tortillas
  Garnishes: guacamole, sliced ripe olives, chopped tomatoes, and sour cream

In a 5-quart pan over medium heat, melt butter. Add eggplant and garlic and cook, stirring often, until eggplant is soft (about 15 minutes). Stir in onion and green pepper and continue cooking for 10 more minutes. Remove from heat and add chiles, 1½ cups of the cheese, and salt and pepper to taste.

In a frying pan, heat enchilada sauce until steamy. Dip each tortilla in sauce to soften; spoon about 3 tablespoons of the eggplant mixture down center of each tortilla. Roll to enclose filling and arrange, seam side down, in a shallow 3-quart casserole or 9 by 13-inch baking dish. Spoon remaining sauce and cheese over tortillas. (At this point you can cover and refrigerate until next day.)

Bake, uncovered, in a 350° oven for about 20 minutes (30 minutes, if refrigerated) or until heated through. Place garnishes in separate bowls to pass at the table. Makes 6 servings.

Stacked Cheese Enchiladas

Tortillas, layered with a cheese-onion filling and covered with enchilada sauce, are baked and then cut into wedges to serve.

  Salad oil or shortening
- 12 corn tortillas
- 1½ cups canned enchilada sauce or red chile sauce
- 2 cups (about 8 oz.) shredded sharp Cheddar cheese or jack cheese
  About 1½ cups chopped green onions (including tops)

Heat a small amount of oil in a wide frying pan over medium heat. Fry tortillas, one at a time, for just a few seconds—tortillas will begin to blister and become soft. *Do not fry until firm or crisp.* Remove with tongs, drain briefly, and set aside.

Dip each tortilla into enchilada sauce, spoon about 2 tablespoons *each* cheese and onion onto tortilla, and cover with a little more sauce. Place in an ungreased shallow 1½-quart casserole or 9-inch-square baking dish.

Repeat with remaining tortillas, carefully stacking one on top of the other. Pour remaining sauce over stack and top with remaining cheese.

Bake, uncovered, in a 350° oven for about 20 minutes or until enchiladas are heated through and cheese is melted. Let stand for 3 to 5 minutes before cutting into wedges. Makes about 4 servings.

Artichoke & Olive Soufflé

This quick and colorful soufflé goes together in minutes with artichoke hearts, olives, jack cheese, and eggs.

    Butter or margarine
    Grated Parmesan cheese
  1 jar (6 oz.) marinated artichoke
    hearts
  1 cup milk
  4 tablespoons butter or margarine
  4 tablespoons all-purpose flour
  ½ teaspoon salt
  1½ cups (about 6 oz.) shredded jack
    cheese
  1 can (2¼ oz.) sliced ripe olives,
    drained
  6 eggs, separated

Preheat oven to 375°. Generously butter a 1½ to 2-quart soufflé dish or casserole. Sprinkle with grated Parmesan cheese, turning dish to coat bottom and sides; set aside.

Drain and reserve marinade from artichokes. Blend 2 tablespoons of the marinade with milk. Coarsely chop artichokes and set aside.

In a 2-quart pan over medium heat, melt the 4 tablespoons butter. Blend in flour and cook, stirring, until bubbly. Gradually pour in milk and continue cooking and stirring until sauce boils and thickens. Add salt, cheese, olives, and artichokes. Stir just until cheese is melted; remove from heat. Add egg yolks, beating vigorously with a wooden spoon.

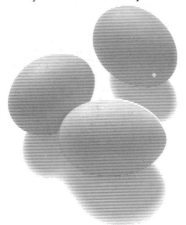

Whip egg whites until stiff, moist peaks form; carefully fold sauce into egg whites. Pour mixture into prepared soufflé dish.

Bake, uncovered, in the preheated 375° oven for about 35 minutes or until a wooden pick inserted in center comes out clean. Serve immediately. Makes 4 servings.

Camembert Soufflé

Just a small wedge of Camembert cheese gives this soufflé an unusually rich taste and creamy texture. It's a perfect choice for a Sunday brunch or for a special late-evening supper served with chilled champagne and fresh fruit.

    Butter or margarine
    Grated Parmesan cheese
  4 tablespoons butter or margarine
  ¼ teaspoon ground nutmeg
  ⅛ teaspoon ground red pepper
    (cayenne)
  3 tablespoons all-purpose flour
  1⅓ cups milk
  2 teaspoons Dijon mustard
  2 tablespoons dry sherry
  4 ounces ripe Camembert cheese,
    rind removed
  1¼ cups (about 5 oz.) shredded
    Gruyère, Samsoe, or Swiss
    cheese
  5 eggs, separated
  ¼ teaspoon *each* cream of tartar
    and salt

Preheat oven to 375°. Generously butter a 2-quart soufflé dish or casserole. Sprinkle with Parmesan cheese, turning dish to coat bottom and sides; set aside.

In a 3-quart pan over medium heat, melt butter. Add nutmeg and red pepper. Blend in flour and cook, stirring, until bubbly. Gradually pour in milk and continue cooking and stirring until sauce boils and thickens. Add mustard, sherry, and the Camembert and Gruyère cheeses; stir just until cheese is melted; remove from heat.

In a small bowl, beat the egg yolks. Gradually stir ¼ cup of the sauce into the egg yolks, then stir mixture back into the sauce. Return to heat and cook, stirring, for 1 minute; set aside.

In a large bowl, combine egg whites, cream of tartar, and salt. Beat until stiff, moist peaks form. Blend ½ cup beaten whites into cheese sauce. Slowly fold sauce into remaining whites. Pour into prepared soufflé dish.

Bake, uncovered, in the preheated 375° oven for 35 to 40 minutes or until top is browned and center feels firm when lightly touched. Serve immediately. Makes about 6 servings.

Cheese-crusted Mushroom Soufflé

A delicate brown crust of Swiss cheese forms on these individual mushroom casseroles. You can use four mini-soufflé dishes (1½-cup size) or one large one.

  5 tablespoons butter or margarine
  ½ pound mushrooms, finely
    chopped
  1 tablespoon chopped green
    onion (including top)
  ½ teaspoon salt
  ¼ teaspoon ground white pepper
    Dash of ground nutmeg
  3 tablespoons all-purpose flour
  1 cup milk
  2 tablespoons dry sherry
  5 eggs, separated
  1¼ cups (about 5 oz.) shredded
    Swiss cheese
    Butter or margarine

Preheat oven to 350° for small soufflés, 375° for large soufflé.

In a wide frying pan over medium-high heat, melt butter. Add mushrooms and onion and cook, stirring, until liquid evaporates (about 5 minutes). Add salt, pepper, and nutmeg. Blend in flour and cook, stirring, until bubbly. Gradually pour in milk and sherry and continue cooking and stirring until sauce boils and

(Continued on page 35)

thickens. Remove from heat and blend in egg yolks, one at a time.

Whip egg whites until stiff, moist peaks form. Fold the beaten egg whites, about 1/3 at a time, into the mushroom mixture just until blended. Then fold in 1 cup of the cheese. Spoon into 4 generously buttered soufflé dishes (1½-cup size) or a 1½-quart soufflé dish. Sprinkle with remaining ¼ cup cheese.

Bake small soufflés in the preheated 350° oven for 25 to 30 minutes, or large soufflé in the preheated 375° oven for 35 to 40 minutes or until puffy and golden and center feels firm when lightly touched. Serve immediately. Makes 4 servings.

Broccoli Soufflé with Cheese Sauce

(Pictured on facing page)

The slight crunch inside this delicious broccoli soufflé comes from sunflower seeds. At the table, pass a colorful Cheddar cheese sauce flavored with mustard and crushed or ground red pepper.

> **Butter or margarine**
> **Grated Parmesan cheese**
> 1 package (10 oz.) frozen chopped broccoli, thawed
> 3 tablespoons *each* butter or margarine and all-purpose flour
> 1 cup milk
> 1 teaspoon salt
> ¼ teaspoon grated nutmeg
> ⅛ teaspoon pepper
> ¼ cup shelled sunflower seeds
> 5 eggs, separated
> About 1 tablespoon shelled sunflower seeds (optional)
> Cheddar cheese sauce (recipe follows)

From oven to table, comes broccoli soufflé with rich Cheddar cheese sauce lightly seasoned with mustard. Recipe is on this page.

Preheat oven to 375°. Generously butter a 1 to 1½-quart soufflé dish or casserole. Sprinkle with Parmesan cheese, turning dish to coat bottom and sides; set aside.

Drain broccoli in colander and press out any excess liquid with a spoon; set aside.

In a 2-quart pan over medium heat, melt the 3 tablespoons butter. Blend in flour and cook, stirring, until bubbly. Gradually pour in milk and continue cooking and stirring until sauce boils and thickens. Stir in salt, nutmeg, pepper, the ¼ cup sunflower seeds, and broccoli; remove from heat. Add egg yolks, beating vigorously with a wooden spoon.

Whip egg whites until stiff, moist peaks form; carefully fold egg whites into sauce. Pour mixture into prepared soufflé dish. If desired, top with about 1 tablespoon sunflower seeds.

Bake, uncovered, in the preheated 375° oven for about 30 minutes or until a wooden pick inserted in center comes out clean. While soufflé bakes, prepare cheese sauce to serve at the table. Serve soufflé immediately. Makes 4 servings.

Cheddar cheese sauce. In a small pan over medium heat, melt 2 tablespoons **butter** or margarine. Blend in 2 tablespoons **all-purpose flour** and cook, stirring, until bubbly. Gradually pour in 1 cup **milk** and continue cooking and stirring until sauce boils and thickens. Add ½ teaspoon *each* **dry mustard** and **salt,** a dash of **ground red pepper** (cayenne), and 1¼ cups (about 5 oz.) shredded **Cheddar cheese.** Stir until cheese is melted.

Chile & Egg Puff

Here's a simple, Mexican-style baked egg casserole featuring diced green chiles, cottage cheese, and jack cheese. Serve with warm flour tortillas and a citrus salad.

> 10 eggs
> ½ cup all-purpose flour
> 1 teaspoon baking powder
> ½ teaspoon salt
> 1 pint cottage cheese
> 4 cups (about 1 lb.) shredded jack cheese
> ½ cup (¼ lb.) butter or margarine, melted and cooled
> 2 cans (4 oz. *each*) diced green chiles, drained
> Butter or margarine

Preheat oven to 350°. In a medium-size bowl, beat eggs until light and lemon colored. Add flour, baking powder, salt, cottage cheese, jack cheese, and butter; blend until smooth. Stir in chiles.

Pour mixture into a well-buttered, shallow 3-quart casserole or 9 by 13-inch baking dish.

Bake, uncovered, in a 350° oven for about 35 minutes or until top is browned and center appears firm. Serve immediately. Makes about 8 servings.

Artichoke & Cheese Custard Squares

Marinated artichoke hearts are baked in a spicy cheese and egg custard mixture. Cool the casserole briefly and then cut into squares to serve.

> 4 jars (6 oz. *each*) marinated artichoke hearts
> 1 large onion, finely chopped
> 2 cloves garlic, minced or pressed
> 8 eggs
> ½ cup fine dry bread crumbs
> ½ teaspoon salt
> ¼ teaspoon *each* pepper, oregano leaves, and liquid hot pepper seasoning
> 4 cups (about 1 lb.) shredded sharp Cheddar cheese
> ¼ cup minced parsley

Drain and reserve marinade from 2 of the jars of artichokes. Into a wide frying pan, drain marinade from 2 remaining jars of artichokes. Chop all artichokes and set aside.

(Continued on next page)

Heat marinade in frying pan over medium heat. Add onion and garlic and cook, stirring, until onion is soft.

In a bowl, beat eggs; stir in crumbs, salt, pepper, oregano, hot pepper seasoning, cheese, and parsley. Add artichokes and onion mixture. Turn into a lightly greased shallow 3-quart casserole or 9 by 13-inch baking dish.

Bake, uncovered, in a 325° oven for 35 to 40 minutes or until center is firm when lightly touched. Let cool in pan briefly, then cut into squares to serve. Makes 6 to 8 servings.

Puffy Sprout Frittata

Crisp bean sprouts abound in this puffy egg frittata. You can also include crumbled, crisply cooked bacon to enhance the flavor.

If you prefer to cook the casserole in one dish, you'll need a wide frying pan with an ovenproof handle. If not, you can start with a regular frying pan and transfer the frittata to a greased and heated shallow 2-quart casserole or 7 by 11-inch baking dish.

- ¾ cup sour cream
- 10 eggs
- 1 teaspoon salt
- ¼ teaspoon ground black pepper
- 2 teaspoons dry basil
- 2 tablespoons chopped parsley
- ⅛ teaspoon ground red pepper (cayenne)
- 3 tablespoons butter or margarine
- ½ cup chopped green onions (including tops)
- ¼ pound mushrooms, sliced
- ½ pound bean sprouts
- 4 or 5 strips bacon, crisply cooked, drained and crumbled (optional)
- ¼ cup grated Parmesan cheese
  Tomato wedges
  Parsley sprigs

In a large bowl, beat sour cream until smooth. Add eggs, one at a time, beating well after each addi-

tion. Stir in salt, black pepper, basil, parsley, and red pepper; set aside.

In an 8 or 10-inch frying pan with an ovenproof handle, melt butter over medium heat. Add onions, mushrooms, and bean sprouts; cook, stirring, until sprouts are tender (about 5 minutes). Stir in egg mixture and crumbled bacon (if desired); sprinkle top with cheese.

Bake, uncovered, in a 375° oven for about 20 minutes or until puffy and center feels firm when lightly touched. Garnish with tomato wedges and parsley. Serve hot or at room temperature. Makes 6 servings.

Brown Rice-Vegetable Casserole with Salsa

Eight garden-fresh vegetables— broccoli, cauliflower, squash, celery, mushrooms, carrots, green onions, and cherry tomatoes— cover a layer of brown rice and green chile salsa. Top with cheese and roasted sunflower seeds for a high-protein, one-dish meal.

- 2½ cups water
- 2 chicken bouillon cubes
- 1 cup brown rice
- 1 bunch (about 1 lb.) broccoli
- 1 small head (about 1 lb.) cauliflower
- 2 medium-size crookneck squash or zucchini
- ¼ cup sliced celery
- ¼ pound mushrooms, sliced
- ¼ cup *each* shredded carrots and chopped green onions (including tops)
- ½ teaspoon soy sauce
- 1 can (about 7 oz.) mild green chile salsa
  About 20 cherry tomatoes
- 3 slices *each* jack and Cheddar cheese (about 8 oz. *total*)
- 3 tablespoons salted roasted sunflower seeds

In a 2-quart pan over high heat, bring water to a boil. Add bouillon cubes and dissolve. Add rice;

cover, reduce heat, and simmer until rice is tender (about 45 minutes). Remove from heat and uncover.

Meanwhile, break broccoli into flowerets with 2 inches of stem; save remainder of stems for other uses. Cut squash into ½-inch-thick slices.

Combine broccoli, cauliflower, squash, and celery; steam over boiling water until vegetables are almost tender (8 to 10 minutes). Add mushrooms. Cover and continue cooking for 2 more minutes. Remove from heat.

Add carrots, green onions, and soy to rice; toss lightly with a fork to combine. Spread rice mixture evenly in a greased shallow 2-quart casserole or 7 by 11-inch baking dish. Spoon salsa evenly over rice and top with steamed vegetables and whole tomatoes. Cut cheese slices in half and arrange halves over vegetables and tomatoes, alternating jack and Cheddar and overlapping edges slightly. (At this point, you may cover and refrigerate until next day.)

Bake, uncovered, in a 350° oven for 15 to 20 minutes (25 to 30 minutes, if refrigerated) or until heated through. Sprinkle with sunflower seeds and serve immediately. Makes 6 servings.

Swiss Chard with Rice & Cheese Stuffing

Hidden inside whole leaves of Swiss chard is an herb-flavored rice and ricotta cheese filling. The dark green bundles bake in a savory tomato sauce made with marinara sauce, parsley, basil, and allspice. Be sure to use large, sturdy, single chard leaves or overlap two small or partial leaves and fill them as one. Briefly steaming the leaves makes them tender but fragile; to make them easier to handle, cool the cooked leaves in a bowl of cold water.

- 1 or 2 bunches (18 to 20 leaves) Swiss chard
- ¼ cup olive oil or salad oil
- ¼ cup chopped almonds
- 2 medium-size onions, chopped
- ¼ cup finely chopped parsley
- 1 teaspoon *each* dry basil and salt
- ½ teaspoon ground allspice
- ⅛ teaspoon pepper
- 1 cup rice
- 2 cups water
- ½ cup chopped celery
- 2 tablespoons lemon juice
- 2 cups (1 lb.) ricotta cheese
  Spicy marinara sauce (recipe follows)
  Grated Parmesan cheese

Wash chard leaves and cut off stems at the base; slice stems and set aside for the filling. Steam leaves over boiling water until leaves are tender but still bright green (7 to 8 minutes). Immediately plunge leaves into a bowl of cold water to cool.

Heat oil in a wide frying pan over medium-high heat. Add almonds, reserved chard stems, and onions; cook, stirring often, for about 5 minutes. Stir in parsley, basil, salt, allspice, pepper, rice, and water. Cover, reduce heat, and simmer until rice is tender (about 20 minutes). Remove from heat and stir in celery, lemon juice, and ricotta cheese.

Carefully separate one chard leaf at a time; lay flat on a clean surface and pat dry. Spoon about

⅓ cup of the rice mixture onto stem end, fold sides in, and roll to enclose filling.

Arrange leaves, seam side down, in a single layer in a shallow 3-quart casserole or 9 by 13-inch baking dish. Prepare spicy marinara sauce; spoon sauce evenly over bundles. (At this point, you may cover and refrigerate until next day.)

Sprinkle Parmesan cheese evenly over top and bake, uncovered, in a 350° oven for about 25 minutes (35 minutes, if refrigerated) or until heated through. Makes about 6 servings.

Spicy marinara sauce. Stir together 1 can (about 16 oz.) **marinara sauce,** 1 clove **garlic** (minced or pressed), ½ teaspoon **dry basil,** a dash of **ground allspice,** and 2 tablespoons finely **chopped parsley.**

Cheese & Mushroom Manicotti

Using canned or prepared spaghetti sauce makes it easy to assemble these cheese-stuffed pasta shells. Everything can be done ahead of time; just allow about an hour for baking.

- 2 cups (about 8 oz.) *each* shredded mozzarella and shredded sharp Cheddar cheese
- ¼ pound mushrooms, coarsely chopped
- 1 can (2¼ oz.) sliced ripe olives, drained
- ¼ cup *each* chopped onion and celery
- ½ cup soft bread crumbs
- 1 egg, lightly beaten
- ¼ cup milk
- 2 tablespoons chopped parsley
- ¼ teaspoon pepper
- 4 cups prepared spaghetti sauce
- 1 cup water
- 8 unfilled manicotti shells
  Grated Parmesan cheese

In a large bowl, combine 1 cup of the mozzarella with Cheddar

cheese, mushrooms, olives, onion, celery, crumbs, egg, milk, parsley, and pepper; set aside.

Combine spaghetti sauce and water; pour half the sauce into a shallow 3-quart casserole or 9 by 13-inch baking dish.

Stuff manicotti shells with cheese mixture and arrange side by side in sauce. Pour remaining sauce over top. (At this point, you may cover and refrigerate until next day.)

Bake, covered, in a 375° oven for about 1 hour. Remove cover, sprinkle with remaining mozzarella, and return to oven, uncovered, for about 10 more minutes or until cheese is melted. Pass Parmesan cheese at the table. Makes 4 servings.

Red Hot Macaroni & Cheese

(Pictured on page 31)

Never before has macaroni and cheese tasted this good! Crushed red pepper, sharp Cheddar cheese, a little Worcestershire and dry white wine, plus rings of bell pepper (if desired) transform the ordinary into the extraordinary.

- 1 pound medium-size elbow macaroni
  Boiling salted water
- ⅓ cup butter or margarine
- 1 medium-size onion, finely chopped
- ½ cup finely chopped celery
- ⅓ cup all-purpose flour
- 2¼ cups milk
- 1 cup whipping cream
- 1 teaspoon *each* crushed, dried red chile peppers and Worcestershire
- 4 cups (1 lb.) shredded sharp Cheddar cheese
- ½ cup dry white wine
  Salt and pepper
- 1 red bell pepper, seeded and cut into rings (optional)

Cook macaroni in boiling salted water according to package directions; drain well and set aside.

(Continued on next page)

Meanwhile, in a wide frying pan over medium heat, melt butter. Add onion and celery and cook until soft. Blend in flour and cook, stirring, until bubbly. Gradually pour in milk and cream and continue cooking and stirring until sauce boils and thickens.

Reduce heat and add red pepper, Worcestershire, and 3 cups of the cheese. Stir until cheese is melted; add wine. Stir in cooked macaroni and season to taste with salt and pepper. Turn into a shallow 3-quart casserole or 9 by 13-inch baking dish. Arrange bell pepper rings on top (if desired), then sprinkle with remaining 1 cup cheese. (At this point, you may cover and refrigerate until next day.)

Bake, uncovered, in a 375° oven for 25 to 30 minutes (35 to 40 minutes, if refrigerated) or until bubbly and lightly browned. Makes about 8 servings.

Ratatouille Cheese Pie

(Pictured on facing page)

Ratatouille— a colorful French vegetable casserole combining eggplant, zucchini, onions, and tomatoes—takes on a new look when shredded Swiss cheese is added and the mixture is baked in a crust. You may wish to decorate the top by arranging the tomatoes in a festive way.

> Pastry dough (recipe follows)
> Flour
> 4 tablespoons butter or margarine
> 1 medium-size onion, chopped
> 2 cups (about 3 medium-size) sliced zucchini
> 1 small eggplant (about ¾ lb.), peeled and diced
> 1 teaspoon dry basil
> ½ teaspoon *each* oregano leaves and salt
> 3 cups (about 12 oz.) shredded Swiss cheese
> 3 medium-size tomatoes, peeled and sliced
> 3 eggs
> ¾ cup milk

Prepare pastry dough as directed. On a well-floured board roll out dough to fit into a 10-inch pie pan or quiche pan. Gently slide into pan. Flute edges, if using pie pan; trim pastry even with top edge of pan, if using quiche pan. Set aside.

In a wide frying pan over medium heat, melt butter. Add onion, zucchini, and eggplant and cook, stirring, for about 5 minutes. Stir in basil, oregano, and salt. Turn into prepared crust, sprinkle with 2 cups of the cheese, and arrange tomato slices on top.

In a small bowl, beat eggs and milk. Pour over tomato slices; top with remaining cheese.

Bake, uncovered, in a 350° oven for about 55 minutes or until lightly browned and a knife inserted just off center comes out clean. Let stand for 10 minutes before cutting in wedges to serve. Makes about 6 servings.

Pastry dough. In a bowl, combine 1½ cups all-purpose **flour** and ¼ teaspoon **salt**. Add 10 tablespoons (¼ lb. plus 2 tablespoons) **butter** or margarine, cut into chunks.

With a pastry blender or 2 knives, cut butter into flour until fine particles are formed. Add 1 **egg** and stir with a fork until dough holds together. Shape into a ball. (At this point you may cover and refrigerate, but bring to room temperature before using.)

Vegetarian's Lasagne

You might not guess that this satisfying, protein-rich vegetable dish is completely meatless. You won't miss the meat with this list of ingredients—whole-wheat noodles, three kinds of cheese, and a thick sauce made with tomatoes, mushrooms, eggplant, and carrots. Bread sticks, a bottle of red wine, and fruit served with an assortment of cheeses would complete the menu.

> ½ cup olive oil or salad oil
> 1 large onion, chopped
> 2 cloves garlic, minced or pressed
> 1 medium-size eggplant (about 1 lb.), diced
> ¼ pound mushrooms, sliced
> 1 can (about 1 lb.) Italian-style tomatoes
> 1 can (8 oz.) tomato sauce
> ½ cup dry red wine
> 1 medium-size carrot, shredded
> ¼ cup chopped parsley
> 2 teaspoons oregano leaves
> 1 teaspoon *each* dry basil and salt
> ¼ teaspoon pepper
> 12 to 16 whole-wheat or regular lasagne noodles
> Boiling salted water
> Butter or margarine
> 2 cups (1 lb.) ricotta cheese
> 2 cups (about 8 oz.) shredded mozzarella cheese
> 1½ cups (about 4 oz.) grated Parmesan cheese

Heat oil in a wide frying pan over medium heat. Add onion, garlic, eggplant, and mushrooms; cook, stirring frequently, for about 15 minutes. Add tomatoes (break up with a spoon) and their liquid, tomato sauce, wine, carrot, parsley, oregano, basil, salt, and pepper; bring to a boil. Cover, reduce heat, and simmer for about 30 minutes. Uncover and continue cooking until sauce thickens (you should have about 5 cups of sauce); set aside.

Meanwhile, cook lasagne in boiling salted water according to package directions. Drain, rinse with cold water, and drain again. Spread about ¼ of the sauce in a buttered, shallow 3-quart casserole or 9 by 13-inch baking dish. Arrange ⅓ of the noodles in an even layer over sauce. Dot noodles with ⅓ of the ricotta. Distribute ⅓ of the mozzarella evenly over ricotta, then sprinkle with ¼ of the Parmesan cheese. Repeat this layering two more times;

(Continued on page 40)

Bright rings of tomato and zucchini slices decorate top of oven-ready ratatouille cheese pie. Recipe is on this page.

spread remaining sauce evenly over top and sprinkle with remaining Parmesan. (At this point, you may cover and refrigerate until next day.)

Bake, uncovered, in a 350° oven for 40 to 50 minutes (about 1 hour, if refrigerated) or until bubbly and heated through. Cut into squares to serve. Makes about 8 servings.

Vegetable Herb Pie

Have you been wanting to try a savory vegetable pie? You're sure to like this one filled with cheese, rice, herbs, and finely chopped vegetables. Serve it barely warm, or pack it in a basket and take it to your favorite picnic site.

    ¼   cup rice
        About ¾ pound *each* zucchini
            and Swiss chard
    2   cups fresh or frozen peas
    ½   cup *total:* finely chopped
            parsley, chopped green
            pepper, and sliced green
            onions (including tops)
    1   small onion, finely chopped
    3   cloves garlic, minced or pressed
    1½ cups (about 6 oz.) shredded
            Swiss cheese
    1   egg, lightly beaten
    2   tablespoons olive oil or salad oil
    1   teaspoon savory leaves
    ½   teaspoon *each* salt, pepper, and
            thyme leaves
        Pastry dough (recipe follows)
    1   egg yolk beaten with 1
            tablespoon water

Place rice in a bowl and cover with warm water; set aside. Finely chop zucchini to make 2 cups. Remove and discard white stalks from chard; chop leaves to make 2 cups.

In a large bowl, combine zucchini, chard, peas, parsley, green pepper, sliced green onion, chopped onion, garlic, cheese, egg, olive oil, savory, salt, pepper, and thyme. Drain rice through a fine wire strainer and add to vegetable mixture; toss gently to mix well.

Prepare pastry dough and divide in half; form 2 balls. Place

1 ball between 2 pieces of lightly floured wax paper and roll into about a 14-inch circle. Line a 10-inch pie pan or quiche pan with pastry, leaving at least 1 inch hanging over pan lip. Fill crust with vegetable mixture.

Roll out remaining dough into a ⅛-inch-thick circle and place over filling. Trim pastry, leaving a 1-inch overhang. Then moisten pastry edges with egg yolk mixture, pinch to seal, and flute edges, if desired. Brush pie crust with egg yolk mixture. Roll out any remaining pastry scraps, cut into decorative shapes, and arrange on crust. Brush again with egg yolk mixture. With a knife, make small slits in crust for steam vents.

Bake, uncovered, in a 400° oven for about 60 minutes (if crust begins to darken excessively, cover loosely with foil during the last 15 minutes). Let cool; serve slightly warm or at room temperature. (At this point, you may cover and refrigerate until next day. Bring to room temperature before serving.) Makes about 6 servings.

Pastry dough. In a small saucepan over low heat, melt ½ cup (¼ lb.) plus 5 tablespoons **butter** or margarine. Remove from heat and stir in ⅓ cup **cold water** and 2½ cups **all-purpose flour.** Mix just until blended.

Swiss Chard & Cheese Pie

(Pictured on page 31)

Slices of hard-cooked eggs are tucked inside this delicious open-faced pie made with Swiss chard, Swiss cheese, ripe olives, mushrooms and sweet, slow-cooked onions. For an added touch, you might want to garnish with rolled anchovies and coarsely ground pepper.

    6   tablespoons olive oil or
            salad oil
    3   large onions, thinly sliced
    1½ teaspoons garlic salt
    1   quart water
    2½ pounds Swiss chard, stems
            removed
        Pastry dough (follow pastry
            dough directions for
            Vegetable Herb Pie, at left)
    3   hard-cooked eggs, sliced
    ¼   cup pitted ripe olives, cut in
            half
    ½   cup sliced mushrooms
    1   cup (4 oz.) shredded Swiss
            cheese
    1   can (about 2 oz.) caper-stuffed,
            rolled anchovies (optional)
    ¼   teaspoon coarsely ground black
            pepper (optional)

Heat 4 tablespoons of the oil in a large frying pan over medium heat. Add onions and cook, covered, until soft. Then uncover, reduce heat, and continue cooking, stirring often, until onions are golden (allow about 30 minutes *total*). Remove onions from heat and stir in garlic salt; set aside.

In a large kettle, bring water to a boil; add chard leaves. Cover and cook over high heat until leaves are tender but still bright green (about 8 minutes). Drain well and set aside.

Prepare pastry dough. Shape into a ball and place between 2 sheets of lightly floured wax paper. Roll out into a ⅛-inch-thick circle, then fit into a 10-inch pie pan and flute edges, if desired. Or fit into a 10-inch quiche dish and trim pastry even with top edge.

Bake crust in a 400° oven for about 15 minutes or until golden brown. Cool slightly on a rack.

Distribute half the chard leaves in crust. Arrange egg slices over chard and spoon onions evenly over all. Arrange remaining chard leaves on top and sprinkle with olives, mushrooms, and cheese. Drizzle pie with remaining 2 tablespoons olive oil or, if desired, drizzle oil from anchovies over pie instead. Garnish top with anchovies and sprinkle with pepper. (At this point, you may cover and refrigerate until next day.)

Bake, uncovered, in a 350° oven for about 15 minutes (20 to 25 minutes, if refrigerated) or until heated through. Serve warm or at room temperature. Makes 4 to 6 servings.

Squash & Spinach Casserole

Spinach, thin slices of crookneck squash, and an herb-flavored, crunchy cottage cheese filling bake together. Toward the end of baking, the casserole is crowned with tomato slices and Cheddar cheese.

    2 cups seasoned croutons,
       coarsely crushed
    ½ pint small curd cottage
       cheese
    ¼ teaspoon *each* dry basil, dry
       rosemary, thyme and oregano
       leaves
    2 bunches (about ¾ lb. *each*)
       spinach, stems removed
    6 tablespoons butter or
       margarine
    6 medium-size crookneck squash,
       cut in ⅛-inch-thick slices
       Salt and pepper
    3 medium-size tomatoes, cut in
       ½-inch-thick slices
    1 cup (about 4 oz.) shredded
       Cheddar cheese

In a bowl, combine crushed croutons, cottage cheese, basil, rosemary, thyme, and oregano; set aside.

Wash, drain, and cut spinach into wide strips. In a wide frying pan over medium-high heat, melt 3 tablespoons of the butter. Add squash and cook, stirring, just until lightly browned. Turn into a shallow 3-quart casserole or 9 by 13-inch baking dish. Sprinkle lightly with salt and pepper; then top with half the crouton mixture.

In frying pan, melt remaining 3 tablespoons butter; add spinach. Cover and cook just until wilted (1 or 2 minutes). Spread spinach evenly in casserole, sprinkle with salt and pepper, and cover with remaining crouton mixture. (At this point, you may cover and refrigerate until next day.)

Bake, uncovered, in a 375° oven for 15 minutes (25 minutes, if refrigerated). Top with tomatoes and Cheddar cheese. Return to oven for 10 to 12 more minutes or until cheese is bubbly. Makes 4 to 6 servings.

Deep-dish Pizzas

You begin these deep-dish pizzas with an herb-flavored whole-wheat crust. Then you spoon the spicy tomato sauce into the crust and top it with your choice of two delicious vegetable fillings.

    1   package active dry yeast
    1¾   cups warm water (about 110°)
    3   tablespoons salad oil
    1   teaspoon *each* garlic salt
         and salt
    1   teaspoon *each* dry basil and
         oregano and savory leaves
    ½   cup wheat germ
    2½   cups whole-wheat flour
         About 2½ cups all-purpose
         flour
         Tomato sauce (recipe follows)
         Vegetable fillings and toppings
         (recipes follow)

In large bowl, dissolve yeast in water. Add oil, garlic salt, salt, basil, oregano, savory, wheat germ, and whole-wheat flour. With a heavy duty mixer, beat at medium speed until smooth (about 5 minutes).

Using a heavy-duty mixer or a wooden spoon, gradually beat in about 2¼ cups all-purpose flour to form a moderately stiff dough. Turn out on a floured board and knead until smooth, adding flour as needed to prevent sticking. Turn dough over in a greased bowl; cover. Let rise in a warm place until size has doubled (about 1 hour).

Punch dough down and divide in half. Pat and stretch each piece of dough to cover the bottom and sides of a well-greased 9 by 13-inch baking dish. Bake on the lowest rack of a 450° oven for about 7 minutes or just until crust starts to brown. During baking, watch carefully and prick any bubbles that form; remove from oven and set aside.

Prepare tomato sauce and your desired filling as directed. Spread half the tomato sauce (about 1½ cups) over each prebaked crust and distribute filling and topping over sauce. Bake on the middle rack of a 450° oven for about 10 minutes or until bubbly and lightly browned. Makes 2 pizzas, each serving about 6.

Tomato sauce. Heat 2 tablespoons **olive oil** or salad oil in a large frying pan over medium heat. Add 1 large, chopped **onion** and cook until soft. Stir in 1 can (15 oz.) **tomato sauce,** 1 can (6 oz.) **tomato paste,** ½ cup **red wine** or water, 1 teaspoon *each* **oregano leaves** and **dry basil,** and ½ teaspoon **salt.** Reduce heat and simmer, uncovered, for 10 minutes.

Zucchini-artichoke filling. Cut 1¼ pounds **zucchini** into strips ¼ inch wide and 2 inches long; you should have about 4 cups. Remove seeds from 1 large **red** or green **bell pepper** and cut into strips. Heat 2 tablespoons **olive oil** or salad oil in a wide frying pan over medium heat. Stir in zucchini and pepper. Cover and cook, stirring occasionally, until tender-crisp (about 8 minutes).

(Continued on page 43)

Uncover and cook, stirring, until liquid has evaporated. Remove pan from heat and stir in 1 cup *each* well drained **ripe olive halves** and sliced **green onions** (including tops); 2 cloves **garlic,** minced or pressed; 1½ teaspoons **oregano leaves;** and ½ teaspoon **pepper.** Mix in ½ cup grated **Parmesan cheese.**

For topping, drain 1 small jar (about 6 oz.) **marinated artichoke hearts** and arrange artichokes over zucchini mixture. Sprinkle with 2 cups (about 8 oz.) shredded **mozzarella cheese.**

Mushroom-onion filling. In a wide frying pan over medium-low heat, melt 4 tablespoons **butter** or margarine. Add 4 large **onions,** thinly sliced and separated into rings. Cook, stirring often, until onions are soft and golden (about 20 minutes). Turn out of pan and reserve.

In the same pan over medium heat, melt 2 more tablespoons **butter** or margarine. Cook 1½ pounds **mushrooms** (cut in halves) until liquid has evaporated. Remove from heat, add reserved onions and ¾ cup chopped **parsley,** ½ teaspoon **salt,** and ½ cup grated **Parmesan cheese.**

For topping, sprinkle 2 cups (8 oz.) shredded **Swiss cheese,** then 1 tablespoon **caraway seeds** over filling.

Baked Lentils with Cheese

Like other members of the legume family, lentils are rich in protein and low in cost. They resemble dried beans or peas but are quicker to prepare since they don't need presoaking. Even after cooking they remain whole, soaking up the good flavors of the other ingredients.

> 1 package (12 oz.) lentils
> 2 cups water
> 1 bay leaf
> 2 teaspoons salt
> ¼ teaspoon *each* pepper, and marjoram, sage, and thyme leaves
> 2 large onions, chopped
> 2 cloves garlic, minced or pressed
> 1 can (1 lb.) tomatoes
> 2 large carrots, sliced ⅛ inch thick
> ½ cup thinly sliced celery
> 1 green pepper, seeded and chopped
> 2 tablespoons chopped parsley
> 3 cups (about 12 oz.) shredded sharp Cheddar cheese

Rinse lentils well under cold water and discard any foreign material.

Pour lentils into a shallow 3-quart casserole or 9 by 13-inch baking dish along with water, bay leaf, salt, pepper, marjoram, sage, thyme, onions, garlic, and tomatoes (break up with a spoon) and their liquid.

Bake, covered, in a 375° oven for 30 minutes. Stir in carrots and celery; return to oven, covered, for about 40 more minutes or until vegetables are tender. Stir in green pepper and parsley; sprinkle cheese on top. Return to oven, uncovered, for 5 more minutes or until cheese is melted. Makes about 6 servings.

Chile Corn Pie with Fresh Tomato Salsa

(Pictured on facing page)

Plump red chile beans, ripe olives, corn, and spicy Mexican seasonings bake underneath a cheese-flavored cornmeal topping in these individual ramekins. Use your own recipe for homemade chile or substitute canned chile beans instead. Our fresh tomato salsa can be made in advance and kept in the refrigerator until mealtime.

> Fresh tomato salsa (recipe follows)
> 8 cups homemade chile or 2 large cans (about 32 oz. *each*) chile beans
> 2 cans (12 oz. *each*) whole kernel corn, drained
> 2 cups pitted ripe olives
> 2 to 3 teaspoons crushed red pepper
> Cornmeal topping (recipe follows)
> Tortilla chips (optional)
> Optional Condiments: tomato wedges, sour cream, avocado slices or quacamole, and fresh coriander or parsley sprigs

Prepare fresh tomato salsa as directed; cover and refrigerate until ready to use.

In a large bowl, combine chile, corn, olives, and red pepper. Spoon mixture, in equal amounts, into 8 individual ramekins (about 2-cups size); set aside.

Prepare cornmeal topping as directed and spoon evenly over bean mixture almost to edges of ramekins.

Bake, uncovered, in a 375° oven for about 25 minutes or until lightly browned. Serve with tomato salsa and, if desired, tortilla chips and optional condiments. Makes 8 servings.

Fresh tomato salsa. Combine 6 peeled and finely chopped **tomatoes,** ½ cup diced **green chiles,** ⅓ cup sliced **green onions** (including tops), 1 teaspoon **salt,** and 1 to 3 tablespoons canned minced **jalapeño chiles** (optional). Cover and refrigerate. Makes about 3 cups.

Cornmeal topping. Scald 1½ cups **milk** with ½ teaspoon **salt** and 2 tablespoons **butter** or margarine. Gradually add ½ cup **cornmeal;** cook, stirring, until thickened. Remove from heat and stir in 1 cup shredded **Cheddar cheese** and 2 **eggs,** beaten.

Individual Mexican ramekin contains meatless chile corn pie served with fresh tomato salsa and crisp tortilla chips. Recipe is on this page.

ETHNIC CUISINE

International dishes with authentic flair

Arroz con Pollo

Seasoned rice, studded with bits of browned pork and onion, combines with tomato chunks and peas in this succulent chicken casserole. The ingredients are cooked together in chicken stock until the rice has absorbed all the liquid.

- ½ pound salt pork, diced
- 2 tablespoons olive oil or salad oil
- 1 broiler-fryer chicken (3 to 3½ lbs.), cut in pieces
- 1 medium-size onion, chopped
- 1 clove garlic, minced or pressed
- 2 large tomatoes (peeled) or 1 cup drained canned tomatoes
- 1 cup rice
- 2 to 2½ cups chicken broth
   Salt and pepper
- 1 package (10 oz.) frozen peas, thawed

In a wide frying pan over medium heat, cook salt pork until well browned; set pork aside and discard drippings.

In same pan, heat oil; add chicken pieces, and cook until well browned. With a slotted spoon, transfer chicken to a shallow 3-quart casserole or 9 by 13-inch baking dish.

Discard all but 2 tablespoons of the pan juices; add onion and gar-lic and cook for about 4 minutes or until onion is soft. Stir in to-matoes, rice, 2 cups of the broth, and browned pork. Bring to a boil and spoon over chicken.

Bake, covered, in a 350° oven (adding broth, if needed) for 45 minutes or until rice is tender and chicken is no longer pink near thigh bone when slashed. Season to taste with salt and pepper. Scatter peas over cooked chicken and rice; return to oven, uncovered, for 5 more minutes. Makes 4 servings.

Beef & Bean Enchiladas

Tucked inside these man-size enchiladas are refried beans, spicy ground beef, onions, and ripe olives. Use canned enchilada sauce and canned green chile salsa to shorten preparation time. Garnish with a single spoonful of sour cream or indulge in the works—green chile salsa, avocado slices or guacamole, tomato wedges, chopped green onion, and extra-spicy chile sauce.

- 1½ pounds lean ground beef
- 1 medium-size onion, chopped
- 1 can (16 oz.) refried beans
- 1 teaspoon salt
- ⅛ teaspoon garlic powder
- ⅓ cup bottled or canned taco sauce
- 1 cup quartered pitted ripe olives
- 12 corn tortillas, at room temperature
   Salad oil or shortening
- 2 cans (10 oz. *each*) enchilada sauce
- 3 cups (12 oz.) shredded Cheddar cheese
   Garnishes: Sour cream, green chile salsa, guacamole or avocado slices, tomato wedges, green onion, or hot chile sauce

In a wide frying pan over medium-high heat, crumble ground beef. Add onion and cook until beef is browned and onion is soft. Stir in beans, salt, garlic powder, taco sauce, and olives. Heat until bubbly, then set aside.

Heat about ⅛-inch of oil in a small frying pan over medium heat. Dip each tortilla into oil for *just a few seconds,* until it begins to blister and become limp. *Do not fry until firm or crisp.* Remove with tongs, drain briefly, and stack; set aside.

Pour 1 can of the enchilada sauce into a shallow 3-quart casserole or 9 by 13-inch baking dish.

Spoon about ⅓ cup of the beef mixture down center of each tortilla and roll to enclose. Place, seam side down, in casserole. Pour other can of enchilada sauce evenly over tortillas; cover with cheese. (At this point you may cool, cover, and refrigerate until next day.)

Bake, uncovered, in a 350° oven for about 20 minutes (35 to 45 minutes, if refrigerated) or until heated through. Garnish each serving as desired. Makes 6 servings.

Chicken Cream Enchiladas

Warm cream cheese blends with bits of chicken, slow-cooked onions, and mellow red peppers in these hearty enchiladas, special enough for a company entrée.

  2 tablespoons butter or margarine
  2 large onions, thinly sliced
  2 cups diced cooked chicken
  ½ cup chopped pimento or roasted sweet red peppers
  2 packages (3 oz. *each*) cream cheese, diced
    Salt
    Salad oil or shortening
 12 corn tortillas
  ⅔ cup whipping cream
  2 cups (8 oz.) shredded jack cheese
    Garnishes: radishes, pitted ripe olives, fresh coriander (cilantro)
    Lime wedges

In a wide frying pan over medium heat, melt butter. Add onions and cook, stirring occasionally, until soft and just beginning to brown (about 20 minutes). Remove from heat and add chicken, pimento, and diced cream cheese. Mix lightly with two forks to blend. Season to taste with salt; set aside.

Heat oil (about ⅛ inch deep) in a small frying pan over medium heat. When oil is hot, dip each tortilla into oil for *just a few seconds* until tortilla begins to blister and

becomes limp. *Do not fry until firm or crisp.* Remove with tongs, drain briefly, and stack.

Spoon about ⅓ cup of the chicken filling down center of each tortilla and roll to enclose. Set enchiladas, seam side down, in a shallow 3-quart casserole or 9 by 13-inch baking dish. (At this point you may cover and refrigerate until next day.)

Spoon whipping cream on enchiladas, then sprinkle evenly with jack cheese. Bake, uncovered, in a 375° oven for 20 minutes or until heated through. (If refrigerated, bake, covered, for 15 minutes; then uncover and bake for 15 more minutes.)

Garnish with radishes, olives, and coriander before serving. Pass lime wedges. Makes 6 servings.

Fiesta Tamale Pie

Here is one of *Sunset's* most requested recipes guaranteed to be a favorite with your family.

  2 tablespoons salad oil
  1 medium-size onion, chopped
  1 clove garlic, minced or pressed
  1 pound lean ground beef
  ½ pound bulk pork sausage
  1 can (28 oz.) tomatoes
  1 can (1 lb.) whole kernel corn, drained
  1 tablespoon chili powder
  ½ teaspoon *each* oregano leaves and ground cumin
  1 cup pitted ripe olives, drained
  2 eggs, lightly beaten
  1 cup *each* milk and cornmeal
 1½ cups (6 oz.) shredded Cheddar cheese

Heat oil in a wide frying pan over medium heat. Add onion and garlic and cook until onion is soft. Crumble beef and sausage into pan and cook until well browned; spoon off and discard excess drippings. Stir in tomatoes (break up with a spoon) and their liquid, corn, chili powder, oregano, and cumin. Cover, reduce heat, and

simmer for 10 minutes; stir in olives.

Spread mixture in a shallow 3-quart casserole or 9 by 13-inch baking dish. In a bowl, combine eggs and milk, then stir in cornmeal; spoon evenly over meat mixture, making sure cornmeal is well distributed. Sprinkle top with cheese.

Bake, uncovered, in a 350° oven for 45 minutes or until top is set and lightly browned. Makes 6 servings.

Baked Chiles Rellenos

Chiles rellenos—"stuffed peppers"—are usually stuffed with cheese, covered with an egg batter, and cooked on the stove; but because our version calls for oven baking, you can assemble it ahead of time. When it comes out of the oven, this soufflélike dish stays puffy for about 5 minutes—just long enough to be garnished and brought to the table.

  2 cans (4 oz. *each*) whole green chiles, drained
  8 ounces jack cheese, cut in strips
    Butter or margarine
  8 eggs
  ⅔ cup milk
  1 cup all-purpose flour
  1 teaspoon baking powder
  2 cups (8 oz.) shredded sharp Cheddar cheese
  1 can (15 oz.) marinara sauce
    Pitted ripe olives

Cut a slit down the side of each chile and gently remove seeds and pith. Fold or stuff equal amounts of cheese inside each chile. Arrange chiles side by side in a lightly buttered shallow 3-quart casserole or 9 by 13-inch baking dish.

With an electric mixer, beat eggs until thick and foamy. Add milk, flour, and baking powder; beat until mixture is smooth. Pour egg batter evenly over chiles and sprinkle with Cheddar cheese.

(Continued on next page)

Bake, uncovered, in a 375° oven for about 30 minutes or until casserole is puffed and jiggles only slightly when gently shaken. Just before casserole is ready, heat marinara sauce to simmering and place in a small serving bowl. Quickly garnish hot casserole with olives and serve at once with marinara sauce. Makes 6 to 8 servings.

Huachinango

Affectionately called *huachinango a la Veracruzana,* this popular Mexican entrée is a spicy tomato and olive-sauced fish specialty from the southern Gulf coast. There are as many versions of this dish as there are chefs who cook it.

Our recipe calls for red snapper fillets that bake in a cinnamon and clove-spiced fresh tomato sauce. Warm flour tortillas and a mixed green salad complement this seafood dish well.

1½ teaspoons *each* lemon juice and water
1 tablespoon cornstarch
2 tablespoons olive oil or salad oil
1 large onion, chopped
2 cloves garlic, minced or pressed
4 teaspoons sugar
1 teaspoon salt
¼ teaspoon *each* ground cinnamon and cloves
5 large tomatoes, peeled and chopped
1 or 2 fresh or canned jalapeño chiles, seeded and finely chopped
2 tablespoons capers (optional)
6 red snapper fillets (about 3½ lbs. *total*) or other rockfish
⅓ cup pimento-stuffed green olives, thinly sliced
3 tablespoons finely chopped fresh coriander (cilantro) or parsley

Combine lemon juice, water, and cornstarch in a small bowl; set aside.

Heat oil in a wide frying pan over medium-high heat; add onion and garlic and cook until onion is soft. Stir in sugar, salt, cinnamon, cloves, and tomatoes. Continue cooking and stirring for about 8 minutes or until mixture boils and thickens. (The thicker the sauce, the better.)

Stir cornstarch mixture and pour into tomato sauce. Cook until mixture boils; remove from heat and stir in chiles and capers (if used).

Arrange fillets in an even layer in a lightly greased shallow 3-quart casserole or 9 by 13-inch baking dish. Pour tomato sauce over top.

Bake, uncovered, in a 400° oven for about 25 minutes or until fish flakes readily when prodded in thickest portion with a fork. Skim any watery juices off sauce with a spoon. Just before serving, gently stir sauce to blend well. Garnish with olives and coriander. Makes 6 servings.

Paella

(Pictured on facing page)

It's been said that classic Spanish *paella*—a potpourri of meats, seafood, vegetables, and saffron-flavored rice—is never the same twice. This is because each region of Spain boasts a different paella. Coastal areas rely heavily on hard-shell clams, mussels, shrimp, and squid, while Inland communities feature paella with tender young chicken or lamb and garden-fresh vegetables such as sweet yellow onions, turnips, and green peas.

Our version combines these and calls for chicken, sausage, scallops, shrimp, clams, and vegetables. To hold all the ingredients, you'll need a paella pan or large wok, or a 14 to 16-inch-wide frying pan with an oven-proof handle.

⅔ cup olive oil or salad oil
4 teaspoons *each* oregano and dry basil
3 cloves garlic, minced or pressed
2 teaspoons salt
1 teaspoon pepper
2 whole chicken breasts (about 1 lb. *each*), boned, skinned, and cut in bite-size pieces
12 large shrimp, shelled (tails left on) and deveined
3 chorizo sausages (3 oz. *each*), casings removed
2 large yellow onions, chopped
1 large green pepper, seeded and chopped
2 cups rice
3 cups hot chicken broth
4 large tomatoes, peeled, seeded, and chopped
½ to 1 teaspoon powdered saffron
1 teaspoon coriander (cilantro)
1 cup fresh peas or 1 package (10 oz.) frozen peas, thawed
½ to ¾ pound scallops, cut in bite-size pieces
12 clams, well scrubbed
2 pimentos, cut in strips (optional)

In a bowl, combine oil, oregano, basil, garlic, salt, and pepper. Place chicken and shrimp in another bowl or heavy plastic bag and pour marinade over them. Cover or seal and refrigerate for at least 4 hours or until next day.

Heat about 3 tablespoons of the marinade in a wide frying pan over medium heat. Leaving shrimp in remaining marinade, remove chicken, drain, and add to pan. Cook until lightly browned; remove chicken and set aside. Cut chorizo into pieces and add to pan; cook over medium heat until well browned. Remove chorizo from pan and set aside.

Add onions and green pepper to pan drippings; raise heat to medium-high, and cook until vegetables are soft. Stir in rice and brown slightly. Add chicken broth, tomatoes, saffron, corian-

(Continued on page 48)

Potpourri of meats, seafood, vegetables, and saffron-flavored rice—that's classic Spanish paella. Recipe is on this page.

... *Paella (cont'd.)*

der, chicken, and chorizo; bring mixture to a boil. Cover, reduce heat, and simmer for 25 minutes, stirring occasionally, or until rice is tender.

Add peas and scallops and toss gently. Transfer paella to a very large ovenproof 6-quart baking dish or paella pan, or 14 to 16-inch ovenproof skillet. Drain shrimp and push into rice mixture along with clams. Bake, covered, in a 350° oven for 15 to 20 minutes or until shrimp turn pink and clams open. Garnish with pimento strips, if desired. Makes 8 servings.

Moussaka Dubrovnik

Our version of moussaka comes from a chef in the town of Dubrovnik, Yugoslavia. This wonderful meat and eggplant dish is made in three steps, any or all of which can be done ahead.

Meat filling
    2 tablespoons butter or margarine
    2 medium-size onions, finely chopped
    1 clove garlic, minced or pressed
    ½ pound lean ground lamb
    ¼ pound *each* lean ground beef and ground pork
    1 egg, lightly beaten
    ¼ teaspoon salt
    ⅛ teaspoon pepper
    2 tablespoons soft bread crumbs

Eggplant mixture
    2 medium-size (1 to 1¼ lbs. *each*) eggplants, peeled and cut lengthwise into ¼-inch-thick slices
       Salt
       Salad oil (about ⅓ cup)
       All-purpose flour
    3 eggs, beaten

Custard topping
    2 tablespoons butter or margarine
    3 tablespoons all-purpose flour
    1 cup milk
    ¼ teaspoon salt
    ⅛ teaspoon ground nutmeg
    2 egg yolks
       Sour cream (optional)

To make meat filling, melt butter in a wide frying pan over medium heat; add onions and garlic and cook until soft. Combine lamb, beef, pork, egg, salt, pepper, and bread crumbs. Stir into onions and cook over medium heat until well browned and crumbly. Drain well and set aside.

To make eggplant mixture, sprinkle eggplant slices with salt and let stand for about 15 minutes. Heat a small amount of oil in a wide frying pan over medium heat. A few slices at a time, dust eggplant with flour, dip in egg, and add to pan; cook until lightly browned on both sides. Add oil if needed. (Slices will be just partially cooked at this point.) Line a shallow 3½ or 4-quart casserole or baking dish with a layer of eggplant, then a layer of the meat mixture. Repeat layers, ending with a top layer of eggplant.

To make custard topping, melt butter in a small pan over medium heat. Add flour and cook, stirring, until bubbly. Gradually stir in milk and continue cooking, stirring constantly, until sauce boils and thickens. Add salt and nutmeg. Remove from heat and stir in egg yolks, beating vigorously with a wooden spoon.

Spoon sauce evenly over eggplant; push eggplant aside slightly to let sauce run to bottom of casserole. (At this point you may cool, cover, and refrigerate until next day.)

Bake, uncovered, in a 375° oven for about 1 hour (70 minutes, if refrigerated) or until bubbly and heated through. Serve with a dollop of sour cream, if desired. Makes 8 servings.

Pastitsio

A unique cinnamon-flavored meat sauce, layered with pasta and topped with custard, characterizes this Greek-inspired casserole. The meat sauce takes time to prepare but the results are well worth it. Extra sauce can be refrigerated in pint containers and frozen for later use. Our recipe can be made ahead of time and refrigerated until baking.

Meat sauce
    3 tablespoons butter or margarine
    3 large onions, finely chopped
    3 pounds lean ground beef
    2 cloves garlic
    1 cinnamon stick
    1½ teaspoons whole mixed pickling spices
    3 cans (6 oz. *each*) tomato paste
    1 tablespoon salt
    ½ teaspoon pepper
    2 cups water

Pasta
    14 ounces large macaroni
       Boiling salted water

Custard sauce
    2 tablespoons *each* butter or margarine and all-purpose flour
    3 cups milk
       Salt
       Freshly ground pepper
    6 eggs

       Butter
    2 cups (6 oz.) grated Romano cheese
    ¼ teaspoon ground cinnamon
       Butter or margarine

To make meat sauce, melt butter in a wide frying pan over medium heat. Add onions and cook until soft. Transfer onion to a 5-quart kettle or Dutch oven. In same pan, cook beef until well browned and crumbly; drain well and add to onions.

In a small cheesecloth bag or large metal tea ball, place garlic cloves, cinnamon stick, and pickling spices. Add to meat mixture along with tomato paste, salt, pepper, and water. Bring to a boil, cover, reduce heat, and simmer, stirring occasionally, for 3 hours or until flavors blend and sauce thickens. Reserve 4 cups for pastitsio. Let remaining sauce cool, remove spice bag, and ladle into pint containers; cover securely and store in refrigerator or freezer.

Cook pasta in boiling salted water according to package directions. Drain, rinse with cold water, and drain again.

To make custard sauce, melt butter in a large pan over medium heat. Blend in flour and cook, stirring, until bubbly. Gradually pour in milk and continue cooking and stirring until sauce boils and thickens slightly. Season to taste with salt and pepper. Whip eggs until light and fluffy; very gradually add hot liquid to eggs, stirring constantly until well blended.

Spoon a third of the pasta into a buttered shallow 4-quart casserole or baking dish. Cover with 2 cups of the meat sauce and sprinkle generously with some of the cheese. Dust with ⅛ teaspoon of the cinnamon. Cover with another third of the pasta and spoon remaining meat sauce over pasta. Sprinkle generously with cheese and top with remaining pasta.

Carefully pour hot custard sauce over pasta and poke with a fork in many places to let sauce run to bottom of pan. Dust top lightly with remaining cinnamon and cheese. (At this point you may cover and refrigerate until next day.)

Bake, uncovered, in a 350° oven for about 40 minutes (55 minutes, if refrigerated) or until bubbly and top is lightly browned. Let cool slightly; cut into squares. Makes 8 servings.

Chicken Cacciatore

In the true Italian style, chicken pieces develop a rich flavor as they simmer in a vegetable-laced sauce of tomatoes, onion, green peppers, and mushrooms. Traditionally, this entrée is served with pasta strands. You might complete the menu with bread sticks, a green salad, fruit, and wine.

¼ cup all-purpose flour
1 teaspoon salt
¼ teaspoon pepper
1 broiler-fryer chicken (3 to 3½ lbs.), cut in pieces
4 tablespoons butter or margarine
½ pound mushrooms, thinly sliced
1 medium-size onion, chopped
2 green peppers, seeded and chopped
2 cloves garlic, minced or pressed
2 tablespoons chopped parsley
½ cup each dry white wine and chicken broth
1 can (6 oz.) tomato paste
¾ teaspoon salt
¼ teaspoon each marjoram, oregano, and thyme leaves
8 ounces spaghetti or fusilli
Boiling salted water
Grated Parmesan cheese

In a small bag, combine flour, salt, and pepper. Shake chicken pieces to coat completely.

In a wide frying pan over medium heat, melt 3 tablespoons of the butter. Add chicken and cook until well browned. With a slotted spoon, transfer chicken to a shallow 3-quart casserole or 9 by 13-inch baking dish. Pour off and discard all but 3 tablespoons of the pan juices.

Add mushrooms, onion, green peppers, and garlic to pan. Cook until onion is soft. Stir in parsley, wine, broth, tomato paste, salt, marjoram, oregano, and thyme; bring to a boil. Cover, reduce heat, and simmer for 10 minutes. Spoon sauce over chicken pieces. (At this point you may cool, cover, and refrigerate until next day.)

Bake, covered, in a 350° oven for 30 minutes; remove cover and

bake for 15 to 20 more minutes or until thigh meat near bone is no longer pink when slashed.

Meanwhile, cook pasta in boiling salted water according to package directions; drain well. Toss with remaining 1 tablespoon butter.

Arrange chicken in center of a deep serving plate, surround with pasta, and spoon sauce over chicken. Pass grated cheese at the table. Makes 4 servings.

Chicken Tetrazzini

Luisa Tetrazzini was considered the greatest coloratura of her time. Today, though, most people recognize her name because of the noodle dish created in her honor.

6 tablespoons butter or margarine
5 tablespoons all-purpose flour
2½ cups chicken broth
1¼ cups half-and-half (light cream)
½ cup dry white wine
¾ cup grated Parmesan cheese
¾ pound mushrooms, sliced
12 ounces spaghetti
Boiling salted water
3 to 4 cups cooked chicken, cut in ½-inch cubes
Salt and white pepper

In a pan over medium heat, melt 3 tablespoons of the butter. Add flour and cook, stirring, until bubbly. Gradually pour in broth, half-and-half, and wine, and continue cooking and stirring until sauce boils and thickens. Add Parmesan cheese and mix just until cheese melts. Remove 1 cup of the sauce and reserve both portions.

In a wide frying pan over medium heat, melt remaining 3 tablespoons butter. Add mushrooms and cook until juices evaporate.

Cook spaghetti in boiling salted water according to package directions; drain well. Combine spaghetti, the larger portion of sauce, mushrooms (reserve a few

(Continued on page 51)

for garnish), and chicken; toss gently. Add salt and pepper to taste. Turn into a shallow greased 2-quart casserole or baking dish. Spoon remaining sauce over top and garnish with reserved mushrooms. (At this point you may cool, cover, and refrigerate until next day.)

Bake, covered, in a 375° oven for 45 minutes (1 hour, if refrigerated) or until bubbly and heated through. Remove cover and broil for a few minutes to brown top lightly. Makes 6 servings.

Lasagne Belmonte

(Pictured on page 31)

Each region of Italy produces its own variation of baked lasagne. This one, features three kinds of cheese, wide noodles, and a thick tomato-flavored meat sauce.

  2 tablespoons olive oil or salad oil
  1 medium-size onion, chopped
1½ pounds lean ground beef
  1 clove garlic, minced or pressed
  2 cans (8 oz. *each*) tomato sauce
  1 can (6 oz.) tomato paste
  ½ cup *each* dry red wine and water
     Salt
  1 teaspoon oregano leaves
  ½ teaspoon *each* pepper and sugar
12 ounces lasagne noodles
     Boiling salted water
     Butter or margarine
  2 cups (1 pound) ricotta cheese or small curd cottage cheese
  ½ pound mozzarella cheese, thinly sliced
  ½ cup grated Parmesan cheese

Heat oil in a wide frying pan over medium heat. Add onion and cook until soft. Add meat and cook until browned and crumbly; discard any fat.

Succulent braised veal shanks simmer on stovetop till tender. Garnish is gremolata—colorful combination of minced parsley, garlic, and zest of lemon. Recipe—called osso buco—is on this page.

Stir in garlic, tomato sauce, tomato paste, wine, water, salt, oregano, pepper, and sugar; bring to a boil. Cover, reduce heat, and simmer for about 1½ hours.

Cook noodles in boiling salted water according to package directions. Drain, rinse with cold water, and drain again. Arrange one-third of the noodles in a crisscross pattern in the bottom of a buttered, shallow 3-quart casserole or 9 by 13-inch baking dish. Spread one-third of the meat sauce over noodles, and top with one-third *each* of the ricotta and mozzarella. Repeat layering, ending with a top layer of cheese. Sprinkle with Parmesan. (At this point you may cool, cover, and refrigerate until next day.)

Bake, uncovered, in a 350° oven for 30 to 40 minutes or until bubbly and heated through. (If refrigerated, bake, covered, for 20 minutes; then remove cover and bake for 30 more minutes.) Makes 6 to 8 servings.

Osso Buco

(Pictured on facing page)

With their succulent treasure of bone marrow, braised veal shanks simmer to perfect tenderness in a delicate, wine-flavored chicken broth. Their sauce is flavored with *gremolata*—the unusual combination of lemon, parsley, and garlic.

  6 tablespoons butter or margarine
  2 large onions, chopped
  1 carrot, finely chopped
  7 to 8 pounds meaty veal shanks with marrow in bones, cut in 2-inch lengths (12 to 18 pieces)
     Salt
     About ½ cup all-purpose flour
1½ cups dry white wine
  ¾ to 1½ cups chicken broth
1½ tablespoons grated lemon peel
  ½ cup minced parsley
  1 clove garlic, minced or pressed

In a very large frying pan (with a lid) or Dutch oven over medium-

high heat, melt 1 tablespoon of the butter. Add onions and carrot and cook until onions are soft. Remove from pan and set aside.

Sprinkle shanks with salt; roll in flour and shake off excess. In pan over medium-high heat, melt remaining 5 tablespoons butter. Cook shanks, a few at a time, until well browned on all sides. (Remove pieces as they brown to prevent crowding.) Return vegetables and meat to pan, standing shanks on end with marrow sides up.

Pour in wine and ¾ cup of the broth; bring to a boil. Cover, reduce heat, and simmer for 2 to 2½ hours or until meat is very tender when pierced. (Or bake, covered, in a 325° oven for 2 to 2½ hours.) If sauce becomes too thick, add more broth. (At this point you may cool, cover, and refrigerate until next day. Spoon off solidified fat.)

Reheat slowly for 30 to 45 minutes, if refrigerated. With a slotted spoon, carefully remove meat and transfer to a warm serving platter; keep hot. Bring sauce to a boil, scraping brown particles free from pan; add broth as needed.

Prepare gremolata by combining lemon peel, parsley, and garlic. Spoon half of the mixture into sauce and simmer for a few minutes. Garnish meat with remaining gremolata. Pour sauce over meat or serve separately. Makes 6 to 8 servings.

Baked Kotleti

Austrians have a simple, yet unusual, way of preparing ground beef. Stiffly beaten egg whites are folded into the meat, resulting in pleasingly light, tender patties that bake in a smooth, creamy sauce. Try serving them with hot buttered noodles or small cooked new potatoes and a green vegetable.

(Continued on next page)

...*Baked Kotleti (cont'd.)*

1½ pounds lean beef
3 tablespoons butter or
  margarine, softened
1 teaspoon salt
¼ teaspoon pepper
1 tablespoon minced parsley
¾ cup soft bread crumbs
2 eggs, separated
2 tablespoons all-purpose flour
¾ cup beef broth
½ cup sour cream or unflavored
  yogurt

In a large bowl, mix together beef,
1 tablespoon of the butter, salt,
pepper, parsley, bread crumbs,
and egg yolks.

Beat egg whites just until stiff,
moist peaks form; fold gently into
meat mixture. Shape meat into 8
to 12 oval patties.

In a wide frying pan over
medium heat, melt remaining 2
tablespoons butter. Add patties
and cook until well browned on
both sides. With a slotted spoon,
transfer meat to a shallow 3-quart
casserole or 9 by 13-inch baking
dish.

Stir flour into pan juices and
cook until bubbly and slightly
browned. Gradually pour in broth
and continue cooking and stirring
until sauce boils and thickens.
Remove from heat, stir in sour
cream, and spoon over patties.
(At this point you may cool, cover,
and refrigerate until next day.)

Bake, uncovered, in a 350° oven
for about 25 minutes (35 minutes,
if refrigerated) or until heated
through. Makes 4 to 6 servings.

Corned Beef & Cabbage

The corned beef for this flavorful
main dish can be cooked up to
two days in advance. Let it cool
and chill in its own broth so it will
retain its juiciness after reheating.

5 pounds corned beef, bottom
  round, or brisket
  About 2 quarts water
1 large onion, chopped
¼ teaspoon *each* garlic powder
  and liquid hot pepper
  seasoning
1 teaspoon dill weed
3 bay leaves
2 cinnamon sticks
5 whole cloves
1 orange, thinly sliced
6 large potatoes
1 large head (about 3 lbs.)
  cabbage, cored

Place meat in a large, 10 to 12-
quart heat-resistant Dutch oven.
Add water and bring to a boil.
Cover, reduce heat, and simmer
for about 30 minutes. (Carefully
taste water—if salty, discard and
add 2 more quarts water to beef.)

Stir in onion, garlic powder, hot
pepper seasoning, dill, bay, cinnamon, cloves, and orange slices.
Bring to a boil. Cover, reduce
heat, and simmer for 3 to 3½
hours longer or until meat is very
tender when pierced. (At this
point you may cool, cover, and refrigerate up to 2 days. Spoon off
solidified fat.)

Reheat meat in broth if refrigerated. Remove meat and strain
liquid through a fine strainer or
colander lined with cheesecloth.
Return broth to pan, add meat,
and bring to a boil.

Cut potatoes in half and carefully drop into boiling broth.
Reduce heat and simmer for 10 to
12 minutes. Cut cabbage into
wedges and carefully drop into
broth; simmer for 5 more minutes.

With a slotted spoon, transfer
meat to a warm serving platter;
arrange potatoes and cabbage
wedges around edges. Pass broth

to spoon over individual servings.
Makes 8 to 10 servings.

Sausages with Sauerkraut

What could be more tempting
than our simplified version of the
popular German dish featuring
sauerkraut, tart apples, and
garlic-flavored kielbasa sausage?
Try making it in individual ramekins, and serve with crusty dark
bread and icy beer.

2 tablespoons butter or
  margarine
1 medium-size onion, finely
  chopped
1 large tart apple, cored and
  diced
1 jar (1 qt.) sauerkraut, well
  drained
¾ teaspoon caraway seeds
1 to 1½ pounds kielbasa,
  knackwurst, or other fully
  cooked sausage

In a wide frying pan over medium
heat, melt butter. Add onion and
apple and cook until onion is soft.
Stir in sauerkraut and caraway
seeds. Turn mixture into a shallow
2-quart casserole or 7 by 11-inch
baking dish.

Diagonally score sausage skins
every inch. Layer sausages over
sauerkraut mixture. Bake,
covered, in a 350° oven for about
20 minutes or until heated
through. Makes 4 to 6 servings.

English Beef & Kidney Pie

(Pictured on page 31)

Hidden beneath a thick, golden
crust of egg pastry lie tender
chunks of beef with lamb kidneys,
diced potatoes, onion, and mushrooms. The ingredients slowly
cook to perfection in a rich,
herb-flavored gravy with a hint
of red wine.

Egg pastry (recipe follows)
1 pound lamb kidneys
⅓ cup all-purpose flour
1½ teaspoons salt
½ teaspoon pepper
1½ teaspoons fines herbes or ¼
teaspoons *each* thyme,
oregano, marjoram, sage
leaves, dry rosemary, and
basil
1½ pounds top sirloin, cut in 1-inch
cubes
4 tablespoons butter or
margarine
1 medium-size onion, chopped
1 pound mushrooms, sliced
1 large potato, peeled and diced
¼ cup dry red wine
1 egg, beaten

Prepare egg pastry.

Split kidneys; remove membrane and center gristle. Cut each kidney into 2 or 3 pieces. Wash in cold water and pat dry.

In a small bag, combine flour, salt, pepper, and fines herbes. Shake pieces of meat and kidneys in bag to coat completely. Shake off excess and set aside.

In a wide frying pan over medium heat, melt butter. Add onion, mushrooms, and potato and cook until onion is soft.

Arrange half of the meat and kidneys in a 2½-quart casserole or baking dish. Cover with half of the vegetables. Add remaining meat and kidneys and top with remaining vegetables. Pour wine evenly over top.

On a floured board, roll pastry out to fit casserole. Roll out pastry trimmings and cut a long strip of dough about ¾ inch wide to fit around rim of casserole. Moisten edge of casserole and press pastry strip onto edge. Place pastry over filling and, moistening edges of strip, fasten firmly onto dough-topped casserole rim; flute edge.

For decoration, roll out scraps of dough and cut leaf-shaped ovals or other fancy shapes, if desired. Prick pastry top in a few places, brush with beaten egg, arrange decorative shapes (if used) on pastry, and brush again with egg. (At this point you may cover and refrigerate until next day.)

Bake, uncovered, in a 350° oven for about 60 minutes (70 minutes, if refrigerated) or until meat is tender. (To test meat, carefully pierce pastry with a long wooden skewer.) Makes 4 to 6 servings.

Egg pastry. In a large bowl, combine 1½ cups **all-purpose flour** and ½ teaspoon **salt.** With a pastry blender or two knives, cut ½ cup (¼ lb.) **butter** or margarine into flour mixture until mixture resembles fine crumbs. Add 1 slightly beaten **egg** and 4 to 5 tablespoons **milk.** Mix with a fork until dough holds together in a ball. Wrap and chill.

Beef Stroganoff with Poppy Seed Noodles

Thin slices of tender beef simmer with onions and mushrooms in this classic entrée from Russia. Since this particular version is baked, it is ideally suited for dinner parties or make-ahead suppers. (A stovetop recipe for skillet Stroganoff appears on page 73.)

Just before serving, add sour cream, then garnish with minced parsley and serve with poppy seed noodles, if you like.

2½ pounds boneless beef round
steak or chuck
Salt and pepper
3 tablespoons butter or
margarine
1 large onion, thinly sliced
¾ pound mushrooms, thinly
sliced
3 tablespoons all-purpose flour
¼ cup tomato paste
1¼ cups beef broth
½ cup dry red wine
¾ teaspoon dill weed
1 clove garlic, minced or pressed
1 cup sour cream
Poppy seed noodles (recipe
follows)
Minced parsley

Cut beef across the grain in ¼-inch-thick slanting slices. Sprinkle with salt and pepper.

In a wide frying pan over medium heat, melt 2 tablespoons of the butter. Add meat and cook until well browned. With a slotted spoon, transfer meat to a 3-quart casserole. Reserve drippings in pan.

In pan with remaining juices, over medium heat, melt remaining 1 tablespoon butter. Add onion and mushrooms and cook until soft. Stir in flour, tomato paste, broth, wine, dill, and garlic. Bring to a boil quickly and pour over meat. (At this point you may cool, cover, and refrigerate until next day.)

Bake, covered, in a 350° oven for about 1¼ hours or until meat is tender when pierced. Remove from oven and slowly stir in sour cream. Serve with poppy seed noodles and sprinkle with parsley. Makes 6 servings.

Poppy seed noodles. Cook 12 ounces of medium-wide **egg noodles** in boiling **salted water** according to package directions; drain well. Toss lightly with 1 tablespoon melted **butter** or margarine and ¾ teaspoon **poppy seeds.**

Hungarian Goulash

Flavored liberally with paprika, this hearty beef and onion stew simmers slowly in the oven for almost 2 hours. Just before serving, you can stir in a cup of sour cream for a rich, thick sauce.

2 tablespoons salad oil
3 large onions, thinly sliced
2 pounds boneless beef chuck,
cut in 1-inch cubes
1 teaspoon *each* salt and caraway
seeds
3 or 4 teaspoons paprika
½ teaspoon marjoram leaves
1 teaspoon vinegar
¾ cup beef broth
½ cup dry red wine or flat
beer
1 cup sour cream (optional)
Additional broth or wine

(Continued on next page)

Heat 1 tablespoon of the oil in a wide frying pan over medium heat. Add onions and cook until soft. Remove from pan and set aside. Add remaining 1 tablespoon oil and cook meat over medium-high heat until well browned. Transfer meat and onions to a 2-quart casserole.

In pan, mix together salt, caraway seeds, paprika, and marjoram; moisten with vinegar and add broth and wine. Quickly bring mixture to a boil and pour over meat.

Bake, covered, in a 375° oven for 1½ to 2 hours or until meat is tender when pierced. (If more liquid is needed during cooking, add broth or wine.) Just before serving, stir in 1 cup sour cream, if desired. Makes 4 to 6 servings.

Boeuf Bourguignon

Burgundy wine, beef, onions, and mushrooms are the essence of this satisfying, hearty stew. You begin this dish on the stovetop, but finish cooking it, untended, in the oven. Accompany with buttered, browned potato slices and a salad to round out the meal.

- 2 tablespoons olive oil or salad oil
- 1 large onion, thinly sliced
- 1½ pounds boneless lean beef, cut in 1-inch cubes
- 2 teaspoons *each* sugar and wine vinegar
- ¾ cup *each* dry Burgundy wine and beef broth
- ¾ teaspoon salt
- ½ teaspoon pepper
- 1 tablespoon butter or margarine
- 1½ pounds mushrooms, sliced
- 1 tablespoon cornstarch blended with ¼ cup water
  Glazed onions

Heat 1 tablespoon of the oil in a wide frying pan over medium heat. Add sliced onion and cook until soft; set aside.

Heat remaining oil in pan over medium heat. Add beef and cook, stirring, until juices evaporate. Stir in sugar and vinegar and cook until meat is browned. With a slotted spoon, transfer meat and onion slices to a 2-quart casserole.

To pan, add wine, broth, salt, and pepper. Bring to a boil, scraping pieces free from bottom of pan; pour into casserole. (At this point you may cool, cover, and refrigerate until next day.)

Bake, covered in a 375° oven for 50 to 55 minutes. Meanwhile, in a wide frying pan over medium-high heat, melt butter. Add mushrooms and cook until juices evaporate; add to casserole. Stir cornstarch mixture into casserole. Cover and return to oven for 20 more minutes. Garnish with glazed onions. Makes 6 servings.

Glazed onions. Peel ½ pound small **white boiling onions** and make crosswise cuts in stem ends. In a pan over medium heat, with **boiling salted water** to cover, cook onions for 20 minutes or until tender when pierced. Drain well, add 1 tablespoon **butter** or margarine, and cook until onions are glazed.

Cassoulet

(Pictured on facing page)

Cassoulet is a popular bean dish from France. Traditionally, the French make it with dried white beans, salt-preserved duck or goose, and a host of other ingredients—depending on the region where the recipe originates. Our version of cassoulet substitutes chicken for duck and adds sausage, ham shanks, and chunks of lamb.

Preparation takes quite a long time, but the generous recipe, serving 8 to 10 people, may be just the right dish for a cold winter evening.

- 2 pounds dry white (great northern) beans
- 4 to 5 quarts water
- 1 tablespoon salt
- 1 teaspoon pepper
- 1 ham shank (about 1½ lbs. with meat on it
- 1 large onion, studded with 6 to 8 whole cloves
- 1 large carrot, cut in thirds
- 6 to 8 sprigs parsley
  About 1 cup celery leaves (attached to stems)
- 1 bay leaf
- 6 chicken thighs (about 1½ to 2 lbs. *total*)
  About 4 tablespoons salad oil
- 2 pounds lamb shoulder (bone in), cut in 2-inch chunks
- 2 bunches leeks (about 1 lb. *each*), trimmed of tough outer layer, green ends removed, and thinly sliced
- 2 cloves garlic, minced or pressed
- 1 carrot, finely chopped
- 1½ pounds kielbasa or other garlic sausage
- 2 cups coarse dry bread crumbs
- 3 tablespoons melted butter or margarine

Rinse beans and drain well; discard any foreign material. Place beans in a 5-quart Dutch oven or large, covered kettle; add water. Cover and bring to a boil. Uncover and boil for 3 minutes; then cover, remove from heat, and let stand for about 1 hour.

To beans and their water, add salt, pepper, ham shank, onion with cloves, 3 carrot chunks, parsley, celery leaves, and bay leaf. Add water (about ½ inch) to cover ingredients, if necessary. Bring to a boil. Partially cover, reduce heat, and simmer for 1½ hours. Remove ham shank. Remove and discard bone; cut meat into bite-size pieces and reserve. Remove and discard onion with cloves, carrot chunks, parsley, celery, and bay leaf.

(Continued on page 56)

Host of fresh ingredients assembled for preparation of cassoulet, a country French baked bean dish. Recipe is on this page.

Meanwhile, arrange chicken thighs in a large greased broiler pan. Place pan about 8 inches from heat and broil for 25 to 30 minutes, turning to brown other side. Let cool, remove meat from bones, and tear meat into bite-size pieces; set aside.

Heat 2 tablespoons of the oil in a wide frying pan over medium heat. Add lamb and cook until well browned on all sides. Remove from pan and set aside. Heat remaining 2 tablespoons oil. Add leeks, garlic, and finely chopped carrot and cook until soft. Remove with a slotted spoon and set aside. Slice sausage in half lengthwise and then into 1-inch chunks. Add to pan juices and cook until well browned (add more oil, if necessary).

To assemble cassoulet, spoon about ⅓ of the beans into a 5-quart casserole or Dutch oven. Add half the leek-carrot mixture, and half of the lamb, the chicken, the sausage, and the ham. Repeat layering, starting with beans; top with remaining ⅓ beans. Combine bread crumbs and melted butter; sprinkle over beans. (At this point you may cover and refrigerate until next day.)

Bake, covered, in a 350° oven for 30 minutes (40 minutes, if refrigerated). Uncover and bake for 30 more minutes or until top is crusty and browned. Let cool for 10 to 15 minutes before serving. Makes 8 to 10 servings.

Basic Crêpes

From France comes a remarkably adaptable entée idea. Crêpes— wafer-thin pancakes wrapped around a delicious filling—are economical and easy to prepare, and the possibilities for fillings are endless.

Here we offer a basic recipe for making crêpes and four recipes for filled crêpes: chicken with artichokes and mushrooms, spinach and onion, seafood, and ham and vegetable.

- 1 cup milk
- 3 eggs
- ⅔ cup all-purpose flour
  About 2 tablespoons butter or margarine

With a wire whip (or in a blender or food processor), blend milk, eggs, and flour until smooth. Place a 6 or 7-inch crêpe pan (or other flat-bottomed frying pan) over medium heat. When pan is hot, add ¼ teaspoon of the butter and swirl to coat the surface. All at once, pour in 1½ to 2 tablespoons batter, quickly tilting pan so batter flows over entire surface. Cook until surface appears dry and edge is lightly browned; turn over with spatula and briefly cook other side. Transfer to a plate and repeat procedure for each crêpe, stacking them when finished. (At this point you may wrap airtight and refrigerate up to one week.) Makes 12 to 16 crêpes.

Freezing crêpes. Unfilled crêpes may be frozen stacked one on top of the other and wrapped airtight. To serve, remove the number of crêpes you need and let them come to room temperature before filling; they tear when cold. Avoid refreezing crêpes.

Filled crêpes may be frozen individually, then baked (without thawing) in whatever quantity is needed. To freeze, place filled crêpes, seam side down and not touching, on a greased baking sheet. Freeze uncovered; then package airtight.

Chicken & Artichoke Crêpes

Chicken, mushrooms and artichoke hearts are blended in a cream sauce.

- 12 to 16 crêpes (see preceding recipe for basic crêpes)
- 5 tablespoons butter or margarine
- 1 small onion, chopped
- ¼ pound mushrooms, sliced
- 3 tablespoons all-purpose flour
- ⅔ cup chicken broth
- ½ cup half-and-half (light cream) or milk
- 2 cups cooked chicken, torn into bite-size pieces
- 1 package (9 oz.) frozen artichoke hearts, thawed, drained, and cut into thirds
- ⅓ cup grated Parmesan cheese
- ¼ teaspoon dry rosemary
- ½ teaspoon salt
  About ¾ cup shredded Swiss cheese

Prepare crêpes or bring to room temperature, if refrigerated. In a wide frying pan over medium heat, melt 2 tablespoons of the butter. Add onion and mushrooms and cook until onion is soft. Add remaining butter and flour and cook, stirring, until bubbly. Gradually pour in broth and cream and continue cooking and stirring until sauce boils and thickens. Remove from heat and stir in chicken, artichokes, Parmesan, rosemary, and salt; cool slightly.

Spoon filling down center of each crêpe and roll to enclose. Arrange crêpes, seam side down, in a shallow casserole. (At this point, you may cool, cover and refrigerate until next day or freeze as directed in Basic Crêpes.)

Bake, covered, in a 375° oven for 20 minutes (30 minutes, if refrigerated; 35 to 40 minutes, if frozen) or until heated through. Remove from oven, uncover, and sprinkle Swiss cheese over crêpes. Return to oven and bake, uncovered, for 5 more minutes or until cheese melts. Makes 6 to 8 servings.

Spinach Onion Crêpes

Here's a meatless crêpe dish that is most satisfying.

- 12 to 16 crêpes (see preceding recipe for basic crêpes)
- 3 tablespoons butter or margarine
- 1 large onion, thinly sliced and separated into rings
- 2 pounds spinach
- ⅔ cup whipping cream
- ½ teaspoon *each* salt and lemon juice
- 2 cups (8 oz.) shredded Swiss cheese
  Buttered mushrooms (recipe follows)
  Sour cream

Prepare crêpes or bring to room temperature, if refrigerated. In a 3-quart heat-resistant casserole or Dutch oven over medium heat, melt butter. Add onion and cook, stirring occasionally, until soft and pale gold (about 30 minutes).

Meanwhile, remove and discard stems from spinach and wash leaves thoroughly; drain briefly and tear into bite-size pieces. Add spinach to onions, cover, and cook for 2 to 3 more minutes or until spinach is limp. Stir in cream, salt, and lemon juice. Raise heat to medium-high and continue cooking and stirring until most of the liquid has evaporated. Distribute filling and cheese among crêpes, spooning it down center of each crêpe and roll to enclose.

Arrange crêpes, seam side down, in a shallow casserole. (At this point you may cool, cover, and refrigerate until next day or freeze as directed in Basic Crêpes.) Bake, covered, in a 375° oven for about 20 minutes (30 minutes, if refrigerated; 35 to 40 minutes, if frozen). Remove cover and bake for 5 more minutes or until edges of crêpes are crisp. Before serving, spoon buttered mushrooms over crêpes; place sour cream in serving container to pass at table. Makes 6 to 8 servings.

Buttered mushrooms. In a wide frying pan over medium-high heat, melt 2 tablespoons **butter** or margarine. Add ¼ pound sliced **mushrooms** and cook until lightly browned.

Tomato Seafood Crêpes

Shrimp and crab bake in a cheese-tomato sauce before being tucked inside the crêpes.

- 12 to 16 crêpes (see preceding recipe for basic crêpes)
- 1 pound medium-size raw shrimp, shelled and deveined
  Boiling salted water
- 2 tablespoons butter or margarine
- 1 medium-size onion
- 1 clove garlic, minced or pressed
- ¼ pound mushrooms, sliced
- ⅛ teaspoon each dry basil and oregano leaves
- 1 can (8 oz.) tomato sauce
- ½ cup parsley
- ½ pound cooked, fresh or canned crab, flaked
- 2 cups (8 oz.) shredded jack cheese
  Sour cream

Prepare crêpes or bring to room temperature, if refrigerated. Cook shrimp in boiling salted water for about 5 minutes or until pink. Drain shrimp well, chop coarsely, and set aside.

In a wide frying pan over medium heat, melt butter. Add onion, garlic, and mushrooms and cook until onion is soft. Stir

in shrimp, basil, oregano, tomato sauce, parsley, and crab. Bring mixture to a simmer, remove from heat, and cool slightly.

Spoon filling and cheese down center of each crêpe and roll to enclose.

Arrange crêpes, seam side down, in a shallow casserole. (At this point you may cool, cover, and refrigerate until next day or freeze as directed in Basic Crêpes.) Bake, covered, in a 375° oven for 20 minutes (30 minutes, if refrigerated; 35 to 40 minutes, if frozen) or until heated through. Remove cover and bake for about 5 more minutes or until edges of crêpes are slightly crisp. Pass sour cream at the table. Makes 6 to 8 servings.

Ham & Vegetable Crêpes

(Pictured on page 31)

Ham, mushrooms, and frozen peas combine in this filling.

- 12 to 16 crêpes (see preceding recipe for basic crêpes)
- 5 tablespoons butter or margarine
- 1 small onion, finely chopped
- ¼ pound mushrooms, thinly sliced
- 3 tablespoons all-purpose flour
- ⅔ cup chicken broth
- ½ cup half-and-half (light cream) or milk
- 2 cups cooked ham, cut in julienne strips
- 1 package (10 oz.) frozen tiny peas, thawed and drained well
- ⅓ cup grated Parmesan cheese
- ½ teaspoon dry rosemary
  Salt
- 1 cup (4 oz.) shredded Swiss cheese

Prepare crêpes or bring to room temperature, if refrigerated. In a wide frying pan over medium heat, melt 2 tablespoons of the butter. Add onion and mushrooms and cook until onion is soft. Add remaining 3 tablespoons butter and flour; cook, stirring

(Continued on page 59)

until bubbly. Gradually pour in broth and half-and-half and continue cooking and stirring until sauce boils and thickens. Add ham and peas. Remove from heat and stir in Parmesan cheese, rosemary, and salt to taste; cool slightly.

Spoon filling down the center of each crêpe (reserve a few mushrooms for garnish) and roll to enclose. (If made ahead, freeze as directed.)

Arrange crêpes, seam side down, in a shallow casserole. (At this point you may cool, cover and refrigerate until next day or freeze as directed in Basic Crêpes.)

Bake, covered, in a 375° oven for 20 minutes (30 minutes, if refrigerated; 35 to 40 minutes, if frozen) or until heated through. Remove from oven, uncover, and sprinkle Swiss cheese over crêpes. Return to oven and bake, uncovered, for 5 more minutes or until cheese melts. Arrange reserved mushrooms on top. Makes 6 to 8 servings.

Pot au Feu

Pot au feu is France's answer to the Italian osso buco—marrow-filled meat shanks that simmer in a delicious broth. But the French go one step further and add meaty beef ribs and garden-fresh vegetables such as new potatoes, leeks, turnips, carrots, and celery root. Although this entrée originates in one pot, the collection of vegetables and ribs is traditionally served on one platter and the savory broth in a separate tureen accompanied by either hot mustard or horseradish.

French entrée coquilles St. Jacques features half shell filled with poached scallops and sliced mushrooms baked in delicate cheese sauce. Recipe is on this page.

4 to 6 marrow-filled beef bones, cut in 3 to 4-inch lengths
6 pounds lean beef short ribs, cut in 3 or 4-inch lengths
3 quarts water
8 to 10 sprigs parsley
1 large onion, studded with 6 whole cloves
4 cloves garlic
1 bay leaf
1 teaspoon *each* salt and thyme leaves
6 medium-size new potatoes, about 1½ inches in diameter
6 small turnips
6 medium-size carrots
1 celery root (optional)
6 leeks
  Prepared hot mustard or prepared hot horseradish

Arrange beef bones in a large, deep, 10 or 12-quart heat-resistant casserole or Dutch oven. Place short ribs on top. Add water, parsley, onion studded with cloves, garlic, bay leaf, salt, and thyme. Bring to a boil. Cover, reduce heat, and simmer for 2 to 2½ hours or until meat is tender.

Meanwhile, scrub potatoes, turnips, and carrots. Peel and cut celery root into sixths. Split tops of leeks down to solid white area and hold them under running water to clean thoroughly. Trim off all but a little green stem.

When meat is tender, add all vegetables except leeks and push them down into liquid. Cover and simmer for 30 to 40 more minutes or until vegetables are tender. During the last 15 minutes, add leeks to meat and vegetables.

With a slotted spoon, carefully lift vegetables and meat from broth and transfer to a warm serving platter; keep hot. If desired, shake marrow from bones onto platter, before discarding bones.

Pour broth through a fine strainer or colander lined with cheesecloth into a tureen; discard seasoning and onion. Skim off and discard fat from broth. Ladle broth into wide bowls. Pass platter of meat and vegetables, or add a selection to each bowl. Accompany with mustard or horseradish. Makes 6 servings.

Coquilles St. Jacques

(Pictured on facing page)

For the French, coquilles St. Jacques is the name of the scallop; for most others, it usually means scallops in a creamy sauce baked and served in large scallop shells or small casseroles.

¾ cup dry white wine
1½ pounds scallops, well rinsed and cut in ¾-inch chunks, if large
3 tablespoons butter or margarine
¾ pound mushrooms, sliced
2 tablespoons all-purpose flour
1¼ cups (5 oz.) shredded Swiss cheese
  Salt
  Minced parsley

In a wide frying pan over medium-high heat, bring wine to a boil. Quickly add scallops; cover and cook for about 3 minutes or until scallops are barely opaque.

With a slotted spoon lift scallops from pan and set aside. Measure poaching liquid; you should have 1 cup. If not, boil to reduce or add water to increase to that amount.

In a frying pan over medium-high heat, melt butter. Add mushrooms and cook until almost all liquid is evaporated. Stir in flour and cook until bubbly. Gradually pour in reserved poaching liquid and continue cooking and stirring until sauce boils and thickens. Stir in 1 cup of the cheese and blend until melted. Add scallops and season to taste with salt.

Spoon mixture in 4 scallop shells or shallow, individual ramekins (about 1 cup size). Sprinkle with remaining ¼ cup cheese. (At this point you may cool, cover, and refrigerate until next day.)

Bake, uncovered, in a 400° oven for 15 to 20 minutes or until sauce bubbles and cheese melts. (If refrigerated, bake, covered, for 10 minutes, then remove cover and bake for 15 more minutes.) Garnish with parsley. Makes 4 servings.

For the

CALORIE-CONSCIOUS

A sleek 450 calories (or fewer) per serving

Meatball Stroganoff with Peppers

You can make these mild-flavored meatballs from ground beef, turkey, or veal. A tangy sour cottage sauce surrounds the meatballs during baking, and bright green or red pepper strips are added at the last minute.

Easy meatballs (recipe follows)
⅔ **cup sour cottage sauce (page 65) or sour half-and-half**
3 **tablespoons** *each* **all-purpose flour and water**
2 **tablespoons margarine or salad oil**
1 **small onion, chopped**
1 **clove garlic, minced or pressed**
1¾ **cups chicken broth**
¼ **cup dry white wine**
½ **teaspoon** *each* **dry basil and oregano leaves**
4 **large green or red bell peppers, seeded and cut into 1 by 2-inch strips**

Prepare meatballs as directed. Place them in a shallow 2-quart casserole or 7 by 11-inch baking dish; set aside.

In a large bowl, combine sour cottage sauce, flour, and water; set aside.

In a wide frying pan over medium heat, melt 1 tablespoon of the margarine; add onion and garlic and cook until onion is soft. Stir in broth, wine, basil, and oregano just until mixture simmers.

Stirring vigorously, gradually add broth mixture to cottage sauce mixture; then pour all back into pan. Continue cooking and stirring until sauce boils and thickens slightly, 2 to 3 minutes. (At this point you may cool, cover, and refrigerate until next day.)

Melt remaining 1 tablespoon margarine in same pan over medium heat; add pepper strips and cook, stirring often, for 5 minutes.

Reheat sauce to boiling; add meatballs and stir gently until hot through. Transfer to a serving platter; arrange pepper strips around edges. Makes 6 servings.

Easy meatballs. In a large bowl, combine 1½ pounds lean **ground veal,** turkey, or beef with ½ cup fine **dry bread crumbs,** 1 small **onion** (chopped), ⅓ cup **buttermilk** or skim milk, 1 clove **garlic** (minced or pressed), 1 teaspoon **salt,** ½ teaspoon **dry basil,** and ¼ teaspoon **pepper.** Mix well and shape into 36 meatballs, each about 1½ inches in diameter. Place in a shallow 2-quart casserole or 7 by 11-inch baking dish.

Bake, uncovered, in a 475° oven for 15 minutes; drain well on paper towels.

Greek Meatballs with Yogurt Sauce

Delicate, mint-flavored beef and lamb meatballs brown in the oven first, then simmer in a light tomato sauce. A parsley-flecked yogurt sauce with a hint of garlic is passed separately at the table to spoon over individual servings.

Yogurt sauce (recipe follows)
1 **pound lean ground beef**
½ **pound lean ground lamb**
1½ **tablespoons finely chopped fresh mint or crumbled dry mint**
½ **cup soft bread crumbs**
2 **eggs**
1 **medium-size onion, finely chopped**
1¼ **teaspoons salt**
⅛ **teaspoon pepper**
½ **teaspoon dry basil**
1 **can (about 15 oz.) tomato sauce**

Prepare yogurt sauce, cover, and refrigerate.

In a large bowl, combine beef, lamb, mint, bread crumbs, eggs, onion, salt, and pepper. Mix well and shape into 18 meatballs, each about 2 inches in diameter. Place in a shallow 3-quart casserole or 9 by 13-inch baking dish.

Bake, uncovered, in a 475° oven for 20 minutes. Remove from oven and reduce temperature to 400°. Drain off pan drippings, if necessary.

Stir basil into tomato sauce and spoon over meatballs. Cover and return to oven for 10 more minutes or until meatballs are done to your liking when slashed. Offer yogurt sauce at the table. Makes 4 to 6 servings.

Yogurt sauce. In a bowl, combine 1 cup unflavored **yogurt,** 1 clove **garlic** (minced or pressed), and ¼ cup chopped **parsley.**

Savory Lamb Ragout

Ragout is the French term for a meat and vegetable stew. Our tempting ragout features chunks of tender lamb, carrots, turnips, and onions that simmer for almost 2 hours in an herb-flavored broth. The result is a rich-tasting yet slimming oven entrée for eight.

  1 tablespon salad oil
  1 medium-size onion, chopped
  2 cloves garlic, minced or pressed
  2 pounds lean lamb, cut in 1½-inch cubes
  1 cup dry white wine
  2 tablespoons tomato paste
  1 cup beef broth
  ½ cup chopped parsley
  1 teaspoon salt
  ⅛ teaspoon pepper
  ½ teaspoon oregano leaves
  ¼ teaspoon dry basil
  6 medium-size carrots
  4 turnips (about 1 lb. total)
 16 small boiling onions
  2 teaspoons butter or margarine
  2 teaspoons cornstarch mixed with 2 teaspoons water

Heat oil in a wide frying pan over medium heat; add onion and gar-

lic and cook until onion is soft. Remove vegetables from pan and reserve.

Add lamb cubes to pan and continue cooking until lightly browned on all sides. Transfer to a 3-quart casserole along with reserved onion and garlic. To pan juices, add wine, tomato paste, broth, parsley, salt, pepper, oregano, and basil; stir together. Raise heat to medium-high, quickly bring mixture to a boil, and pour over meat. Cover and bake in a 375° oven for 1 hour.

Meanwhile, cut carrots and turnips into 1-inch chunks; leave onions whole. Melt butter in same frying pan over medium heat; add carrots, turnips, and onions and cook until vegetables are glazed and lightly browned; set aside.

Stir a little lamb broth into cornstarch mixture, then pour mixture over lamb. Gently stir in vegetables. Cover and return to oven for about 50 minutes longer or until lamb and vegetables are tender when pierced. Makes 8 servings.

Orange Chicken with Carrots

Frozen orange juice concentrate is the secret ingredient in this simple, colorful baked chicken and carrot combination. To round out this low calorie meal, offer a salad of crisp greens and sliced cucumbers tossed with a simple lemon juice dressing.

  1 broiler-fryer chicken (3 to 3½ lbs.), cut in pieces and skinned
  5 or 6 medium-size carrots, diagonally cut in ½-inch-thick slices
  1 can (6 oz.) frozen orange juice concentrate, thawed
  2 tablespoons cornstarch
  ½ teaspoon salt
  ⅛ teaspoon white pepper
  ¼ cup chopped green onions (including tops)

Arrange chicken in a shallow 3-quart casserole or 9 by 13-inch baking dish. Scatter carrots over top.

Combine orange juice, cornstarch, salt, and pepper; spoon over carrots and chicken.

Cover and bake in a 375° oven for 45 minutes. Remove from oven, carefully baste with pan juices, and sprinkle with onion. Cover and return to oven for about 15 more minutes or until meat near thigh bone is no longer pink when slashed. Makes 4 to 6 servings.

Chicken & Vegetables in Wine

French cuisine traditionally offers coq au vin (see page 17), combining chicken and vegetables with a dry red wine. Our recipe calls for dry white wine, and the result is a richly aromatic and equally flavorful variation.

  1 tablespoon salad oil
  1 broiler-fryer chicken (3 to 3½ lbs.), cut in pieces
  1 tablespoon chopped parsley
  ½ teaspoon poultry seasoning
  1 teaspoon salt
  1 clove garlic, minced or pressed
  ½ pound small whole mushrooms
  1 large carrot, diagonally cut in ¼-inch-thick slices
  1 package (10 oz.) frozen boiling onions, thawed, or ½ pound small boiling onions
  1 cup dry white wine
  1 teaspoon cornstarch combined with 1 teaspoon water

Heat oil in a wide frying pan over medium heat; add chicken and cook until lightly browned on all sides. Transfer chicken to a 3-quart casserole or Dutch oven, but reserve pan juices. Sprinkle chicken with parsley, poultry seasoning, and salt; set aside.

To pan juices, add garlic, mushrooms, and carrot. Cook just until vegetables are glazed (about 2 minutes); stir in onions. Spoon vegetables over chicken and add wine.

Cover and bake in a 375° oven for 40 minutes. Remove casserole from oven. Carefully, take some of the hot wine broth from casserole and stir into cornstarch mixture. Pour mixture back into casserole and stir gently to mix well.

Return to oven and bake, uncovered, for 15 to 20 more minutes or until meat near thigh bone is no longer pink when slashed. Makes 4 servings.

Lemon Chicken

(Pictured on facing page)

Here's one of our easiest, most requested recipes for chicken. The flavoring—definitely lemon—is a tart-sweet combination of lemon peel and juice, thin lemon slices, and brown sugar. Serve this casserole with a leafy green vegetable such as spinach or chard.

  2 large lemons
  8 pieces (breasts, legs,thighs)
      broiler-fryer chicken (about 3
      lbs. *total*)
 ⅓ cup all-purpose flour
  1 teaspoon salt
 ½ teaspoon paprika
  4 tablespoons salad oil or
      shortening
  2 tablespoons brown sugar
  1 cup chicken broth
      Mint sprig (optional)

Grate and reserve peel from 1 of the lemons, then cut lemon in half and squeeze juice over chicken pieces; thoroughly coat each piece with juice. In a small bag, combine flour, salt, and paprika. Place chicken, a few pieces at a time, in bag and shake to coat completely.

Heat oil in a wide frying pan over medium heat. Add chicken and cook until well browned on all sides. Transfer chicken to a shallow 3-quart casserole or 9 by 13-inch baking dish.

Sprinkle reserved lemon peel and brown sugar over chicken.

Cut second lemon into thin slices and arrange over chicken; pour broth over chicken.

Bake, covered, in a 375° oven for 40 to 45 minutes or until meat near bone is no longer pink when slashed. Garnish with mint, if desired. Makes 4 to 6 servings.

Oriental Chicken

Chicken breasts marinate in a soy and sherry mixture flavored with a hint of garlic and fresh ginger. You'll need to reserve part of the marinade for cooking the vegetables, which are slightly stir-fried and then added at the last minute.

 ¼ cup soy sauce
  1 tablespoon dry sherry
  1 teaspoon minced fresh ginger
      or ½ teaspoon ground ginger
  1 large clove garlic, minced or
      pressed
  3 whole chicken breasts (about 1
      lb. *each*), split, skinned, and
      boned
 ⅓ cup chicken broth
  2 teaspoons cornstarch
  1 teaspoon salad oil
  2 large green peppers, seeded and
      cut in 1-inch squares
  2 stalks celery, diagonally cut in
      ½-inch-thick slices
  1 can (4 to 6 oz.) water chestnuts,
      drained and sliced
  1 can (8 oz.) juice-packed
      pineapple chunks, drained
      well

In a bowl, combine soy sauce, sherry, ginger, and garlic. Place chicken in a heavy plastic bag or large bowl. Pour marinade over chicken, cover, and refrigerate for 4 hours, turning occasionally.

Lift chicken from marinade and transfer to a shallow 2-quart casserole or 7 by 11-inch baking dish. Reserve 2 tablespoons of the marinade; discard the remainder. Cover and bake chicken in a 325° oven for about 35 minutes. Remove from oven, drain off juices, and set chicken aside.

Add broth and cornstarch to reserved 2 tablespoons marinade

and set aside. Heat oil in a wide frying pan over medium heat; add peppers, celery, water chestnuts, and pineapple; stir-fry just until pieces are glazed (about 2 minutes).

Stir broth mixture once or twice and gradually pour into vegetables, cooking and stirring until sauce thickens. Spoon over chicken, cover, and return casserole to oven for 15 more minutes or until meat near thigh bone is no longer pink when slashed. Makes 6 servings.

Chicken & Artichoke Hearts

If you're searching for an elegant party dish, try this simple, delicious chicken and artichoke combination. It's an excellent choice when you're having guests, because you can prepare it ahead and bake it just before they arrive. Serve with a flavored rice and a salad with a zesty oil and vinegar dressing.

  1 broiler-fryer chicken (3 to 3½
      lbs.), cut in pieces and
      skinned
  2 packages (9 oz. *each*) frozen
      artichoke hearts, thawed and
      cut into quarters
  2 tablespoons cornstarch
  1 teaspoon salt
 ½ teaspoon *each* garlic powder
      and paprika
 ¼ teaspoon *each* white pepper and
      dry rosemary
 ⅔ cup chicken broth
  3 tablespoons dry sherry
  2 tablespoons butter or
      margarine
 ¼ pound mushrooms, sliced

Arrange chicken in a lightly greased, shallow 3-quart casserole

(Continued on page 64)

Just two lemons plus a touch of brown sugar create tart-sweet flavoring for low-calorie chicken casserole. Recipe for lemon chicken is on this page.

or 9 by 13-inch baking dish. Top with artichoke pieces.

In a bowl, combine cornstarch, salt, garlic powder, paprika, pepper, rosemary, chicken broth, and sherry; set aside.

In a medium-size frying pan over medium heat, melt butter; add mushrooms and cook until barely tender. Stir cornstarch mixture, add to mushrooms, and cook, stirring, until sauce boils and thickens slightly; then pour over artichokes. (At this point you may cover and refrigerate until next day.)

Bake, covered, in a 375° oven for 1 hour (1¼ hours, if refrigerated) or until meat near thigh bone is no longer pink when slashed. Makes 4 to 6 servings.

Baked Turkey Legs & Vegetables

Turkey can help trim the budget as well as the waistline, so why not take advantage of this double incentive by preparing a turkey casserole? Our quick and easy turkey bake features carrots, celery, onion, and diced potato cooked in a little chicken broth and white wine.

- 4 **turkey drumsticks or 2 drumsticks and 2 thighs (3 to 3½ lbs.** *total***)**
- ½ **cup** *each* **chicken broth and dry white wine**
- ¼ **teaspoon** *each* **pepper and paprika**
- 1 **teaspoon salt**
- 1 **tablespoon** *each* **cornstarch and salad oil**
- 1 **clove garlic, minced or pressed**
- 1 **large onion, sliced and separated into rings**
- 2 **large carrots, diagonally cut into ¼-inch-thick slices**
- 2 **stalks celery, diagonally cut into ¼-inch-thick slices**
- 1 **large potato**

Remove and discard skin from turkey. Arrange turkey in a shal-

low 3-quart casserole or 9 by 13-inch baking dish.

In a small bowl, combine broth, wine, pepper, paprika, salt, and cornstarch; set aside.

Heat oil in a wide frying pan over medium heat; add garlic and onion and cook until onion is soft. Stir in carrots and celery; continue cooking and stirring for about 5 minutes. Stir broth-wine mixture, gradually pour into pan, and continue cooking until it boils and thickens slightly. Spoon over turkey legs. (At this point you may cover and refrigerate until next day.)

Bake, covered, in a 350° oven for about 1 hour. Meanwhile, peel and dice potato. Remove casserole from oven, and stir diced potato into broth. Cover casserole and return to oven for about 1 hour more or until meat near bone is no longer pink when slashed. Makes 4 servings.

Fish Fillets Italiano

Tender fish fillets—cod, sole, perch, or haddock—bake in a vegetable-laced tomato sauce in about 30 minutes. This recipe calls for ready-to-cook fish that have been boned, skinned, and then frozen in block packages.

- 1 **tablespoon salad oil**
- 1 **clove garlic, minced or pressed**
- ¼ **cup chopped onion**
- ¼ **pound mushrooms, chopped**
- 2 **medium-size zucchini, diced**
- 1 **can (15 oz.) tomato sauce**
- ¾ **teaspoon** *each* **dry basil and oregano leaves**
- ¼ **teaspoon salt Pepper to taste**
- 1 **package (about 1 lb.) frozen fish fillets, thawed**
- ¾ **cup shredded mozzarella cheese (made from part skim milk)**

Heat oil in a wide frying pan over medium heat; add garlic and onion and cook until onion is soft.

Stir in mushrooms and zucchini and continue cooking and stirring for about 8 minutes or until mushrooms are soft.

Add tomato sauce, basil, oregano, salt, and pepper. Bring to a boil, then reduce heat and simmer for about 15 minutes or until sauce boils and thickens slightly.

Arrange fillets in an even layer in a lightly greased shallow 2-quart casserole or 7 by 11-inch baking dish. Spoon hot sauce over fillets.

Bake, uncovered, in a 350° oven for about 25 minutes or until fish flakes readily when prodded in thickest portion with a fork. Remove from oven, sprinkle cheese over fillets, and return to oven for 5 minutes longer or until cheese melts. Makes 4 servings.

Cheese-topped Fish Fillets

A savory Cheddar cheese and vegetable sauce bakes atop fish fillets in this easy-to-make dinner entrée. You can choose from a number of white-fleshed fish—sole, lingcod, halibut, or perch.

- 2 **pounds fish fillets (see suggestions above)**
- 1 **tablespoon butter or margarine**
- ¼ **pound mushrooms, sliced**
- 2 **tablespoons minced green onion (including tops)**
- ¾ **teaspoon salt**
- ¼ **teaspoon pepper**
- ½ **teaspoon dry basil**
- 1 **medium-size tomato, peeled, seeded, and chopped**
- 1 **cup (4 oz.) shredded Cheddar cheese**
- 1 **egg**

Lightly grease a shallow 2-quart casserole or 7 by 11-inch baking dish and arrange fish in it in an even layer. Bake, uncovered, in a 400° oven for 10 minutes.

Meanwhile, in a wide frying pan over medium heat, melt but-

(Continued on page 67)

Delectable sauces for the diet-conscious cook

Sour Cottage Sauce

Cream sauces are usually a "no-no" for the calorie-conscious. The creamy sauces on this page, though, are made with a sour cream substitute you make yourself by whirling cottage cheese in a food processor or blender.

  1 **pint (2 cups) large curd cottage cheese**
 ¼ **cup skim milk**
  2 **tablespoons lemon juice**

Turn cottage cheese into a fine wire strainer. Hold under cold running water and stir gently with a rubber scraper until water runs clear; drain for about 20 minutes.

   Put cottage cheese, milk, and lemon juice into a food processor or blender. Whirl until completely smooth, stopping as needed to push mixture into blades and to taste for graininess (this takes about 5 minutes). Cover and refrigerate (it keeps as long as cottage cheese). Makes about 1⅓ cups.

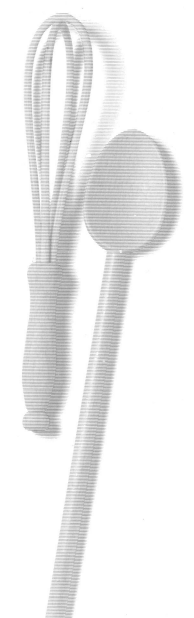

Mushroom-Wine Sauce

Flavored with just a hint of Dijon mustard, this mushroom-wine sauce is rich tasting, even though it's made without butter or cream.

  1 **tablespoon** *each* **margarine and salad oil**
 ½ **pound mushrooms, sliced**
  1 **small onion, chopped**
  1 **clove garlic, minced or pressed**
 ¾ **cup chicken broth**
 ¼ **cup dry white wine or additional chicken broth**
 ½ **teaspoon thyme leaves**
  1 **teaspoon Dijon mustard**
 ⅔ **cup sour cottage sauce (see previous recipe)**
  2 **tablespoons** *each* **all-purpose flour and water**
    Salt and pepper

Heat margarine and oil in a wide frying pan over medium heat. Add mushrooms, onion, and garlic; cook, stirring, until onion is soft. Add broth, wine, thyme, and mustard. Bring to a simmer.

   In a large bowl, combine sour cottage sauce with flour and water mixture until smooth. Stirring vigorously, gradually pour hot liquid into sour cottage sauce mixture, then return to pan. Bring to a boil, stirring constantly and continue boiling and stirring for 2 to 3 minutes. Season to taste with salt and pepper. Makes about 2 cups.

Tartar Sauce

Chopped dill pickle, minced green onion, capers, and Dijon mustard are featured in this tasty tartar sauce. Despite its low-calorie content, it adds rich flavor to all types of fish. It can be stored, covered, in the refrigerator for up to one week.

  2 **to 4 tablespoons mayonnaise (or low-calorie mayonnaise)**
    About 1 cup sour cottage sauce (recipe on this page)
  2 **teaspoons** *each* **Dijon mustard and prepared horseradish (or omit horseradish and use 1 tablespoon Dijon mustard)**
 ¼ **cup finely chopped dill pickle**
  2 **tablespoons minced green onions (including tops)**
  1 **teaspoon capers, drained and chopped (or 1 teaspoon dill weed)**
    Garlic salt and pepper

Place 2 to 4 tablespoons mayonnaise in a measuring cup and add enough sour cottage sauce to make 1 cup. Stir in mustard, horseradish, dill pickle, onion, and capers; mix well. Season to taste with garlic salt and pepper. Makes about 1⅓ cups.

ter; add mushrooms and onion and cook until most of the liquid has evaporated. Remove from heat and stir in salt, pepper, basil, tomato, and cheese. Remove fish from oven and reduce temperature to 350°. Spoon onion mixture evenly over fillets.

Return to oven and bake, uncovered, for 20 minutes or until fish flakes readily when prodded in thickest portion with a fork. Makes 6 servings.

Sole Florentine

(Pictured on facing page)

Rolled-up sole fillets, stuffed with a lemon-spinach filling , are gently poached in clam juice and white wine, then arranged on a bed of shredded spinach. We offer a delicate, low-calorie sour cream sauce to serve alongside, but you can prepare this dish without it.

- 1 **package (10 oz.) frozen chopped spinach, thawed**
- 6 **sole fillets (about 2 lbs.** *total***)**
- ½ **teaspoon salt**
- ¼ **teaspoon ground nutmeg**
- 2 **tablespoons** *each* **grated lemon peel and chopped parsley**
- 1 **bottle (8 oz.) clam juice**
- ½ **cup dry white wine**
- 1 **small bay leaf**
- 4 **or 5 whole black peppers (peppercorns)**
- 2 **bunches (about 1 lb.** *each***) spinach, washed, drained, and coarsely shredded**
   Optional lemon sour cream sauce (recipe follows)
   Lemon twists (optional)

Squeeze out excess moisture from chopped spinach and place in a small bowl.

Trim each fish fillet into a rectangle measuring about 3 by 8 inches (reserve trimmings); set aside. Finely chop reserved

trimmings. In a bowl, combine chopped fish with chopped spinach. Add salt, nutmeg, lemon peel, and parsley; mix well.

Spread about 3 tablespoons of the fish-spinach mixture over each fillet; gently roll up fillet and secure with a wooden pick. (At this point you may cover and refrigerate for 1 to 2 hours.)

In a wide frying pan over medium heat, place clam juice, wine, bay leaf, and whole peppers. Bring mixture to a boil, then carefully add fish fillets. Cover, reduce heat, and simmer for 4 minutes or until fish begins to become opaque *(do not overcook)*.

Meanwhile, spread shredded spinach in a shallow 3-quart casserole or 9 by 13-inch baking dish. With a slotted spoon, lift fish from pan (reserve poaching liquid for lemon sour cream sauce) and arrange on top of spinach.

Bake, covered, in a 325° oven for 15 to 20 minutes or until fish flakes easily when prodded with a fork. While fish bakes, prepare lemon sauce, if desired. Garnish individual servings with lemon twist, if desired, and offer sauce at the table. Makes 6 servings.

Lemon sour cream sauce. In a large bowl, combine ⅔ cup **sour cottage sauce** (recipe on page 65) with 2 tablespoons **cornstarch** dissolved in 2 tablespoons **water.** Strain and measure reserved **poaching broth** into a pan, adding water, if necessary, to make 1½ cups. Bring broth to a simmer over medium heat. Stirring vigorously, gradually pour hot broth into sour cottage sauce mixture, then return to pan. Continue cooking and stirring until sauce boils and thickens.

Shrimp with Wild Rice

Such choice foods as wild rice, shrimp, and plump mushroom caps make this impressive casserole fit for a company buffet.

- 1 **package (about 6 oz.) wild and long grain rice mix**
   Boiling salted water
- 1 **pound mushrooms**
- 2 **tablespoons butter or margarine**
- 1 **medium-size onion, finely chopped**
- 1 **tablespoon** *each* **lemon juice and all-purpose flour**
- 1¼ **cups chicken broth**
- ½ **cup dry white wine**
- ½ **teaspoon** *each* **salt and tarragon**
- ¼ **teaspoon garlic salt**
- 3 **tablespoons grated Parmesan cheese**
- 1½ **pounds medium-size shrimp, cooked, shelled, and deveined**
- 1 **tablespoon finely chopped parsley**

Cook rice in boiling salted water according to package directions; set aside.

Wash mushrooms. Remove and chop stems; set caps aside.

In a wide frying pan over medium heat, melt 1 tablespoon of the butter; add mushroom stems and onion and cook until soft. Add mushroom caps and sprinkle with lemon juice. Stirring gently, continue cooking until mushroom caps are soft.

Melt remaining 1 tablespoon butter in same pan, stir in flour, and cook until bubbly. Gradually pour in chicken broth and wine and cook, stirring, until sauce boils and thickens slightly. Stir in salt, tarragon, garlic salt, and cheese. Reserve ¼ cup of the sauce.

Mix together remaining sauce, rice, mushroom mixture, and shrimp (reserving a few shrimp for garnish). Spoon into a lightly greased 2-quart casserole, arrange reserved shrimp on top, and spoon over the reserved ¼ cup sauce. (At this point you may cool, cover, and refrigerate until next day.)

Bake, covered, in a 350° oven for 25 minutes (35 to 40 minutes, if refrigerated) or until hot through. Garnish with chopped parsley. Makes 6 servings.

Rolled-up fish fillets show off spirals of lemon-spinach stuffing. Rolls are poached, then baked atop a bed of shredded spinach. Recipe is on this page.

STOVETOP SPECIALTIES

One-dish skillet meals, ready in minutes

Ground Beef Curry

Here's a quick recipe for curry that substitutes ground beef for the more traditional chicken or lamb. Your guests will enjoy individualizing their servings by choosing from among a wide assortment of garnishes.

1 tablespoon salad oil
1 medium-size onion, chopped
1 pound lean ground beef
1 package (1¾ oz.) pine nuts
1½ teaspoons curry powder
¼ teaspoon garlic salt
   Salt and pepper
1 can (8 oz.) tomato sauce
1 cup water
¼ cup finely chopped parsley
   About 4 cups hot cooked rice or bulgur wheat
   Assorted condiments: sliced green onions (including tops), crisp bacon (crumbled), raisins, salted cashews, chopped cucumber, shredded coconut

Heat oil in a wide frying pan over medium heat. Add onion and cook until soft. Add ground beef and cook until well browned and crumbly; stir in pine nuts, curry powder, garlic salt, salt and pepper to taste, tomato sauce, and water. Bring to a boil. Reduce heat and simmer until sauce begins to thicken slightly (about 5 minutes).

Just before serving, stir in parsley. Serve over rice and pass condiments at the table. Makes 4 servings.

Piperade with Bacon & Vegetables

Piperade is a colorful, Basque-style flat omelet that is filled, in this case, with bacon, peppers, and tomatoes.

4 slices bacon, cut in small pieces
2 small green peppers, seeded and cut in julienne strips
2 medium-size tomatoes, peeled, seeded, and diced
2 cups (about ½ lb.) cooked ham, coarsely chopped
¼ cup chopped parsley
16 eggs
¼ cup water
1 teaspoon salt
¼ teaspoon pepper

In a 12 or 14-inch frying pan over medium-low heat, cook bacon until crisp and browned. With a slotted spoon, remove bacon and set aside.

Raise heat to medium and add green pepper to pan drippings. Cook pepper until soft but still bright green. Stir in tomatoes, ham, and parsley; cook until heated through. With a slotted spoon, remove vegetable-ham mixture and set aside; keep warm.

Combine eggs, water, salt, and pepper; mix well. Pour into frying pan, reduce heat to low, and cook eggs, gently lifting cooked portion to allow uncooked portion to flow underneath. When eggs are almost set, distribute vegetables and ham over surface and continue cooking, gently shaking pan, until eggs are set to your liking. Sprinkle with bacon and serve from pan. Makes 6 to 8 servings.

Potato-Sausage Supper

Sausage, potatoes, celery, onion, and dill pickle make a hearty combination in this one-dish meal. Any fully cooked sausage —kielbasa, frankfurters, or smoked sausage links—can be used.

1 pound fully cooked sausage,
   thinly sliced
1½ pounds boiling potatoes
   (unpeeled)
   About 6 tablespoons butter or
   margarine
1 large onion, sliced
½ cup *each* chopped celery and
   dill pickle
¾ cup dill pickle liquid
1 tablespoon sugar
½ teaspoon *each* caraway seeds
   and dry mustard
   Salt and pepper
   Chopped parsley

In a wide frying pan over medium
heat, cook sausage until browned.
With a slotted spoon, remove sausage and set aside.

Cut unpeeled potatoes into
¼-inch-thick slices. In same pan,
melt 3 tablespoons of the butter.
Add potato slices, a few at a time,
to be sure each slice gets coated
with butter, and turn frequently,
adding more butter as needed to
coat potatoes thoroughly. Add
onion and cook, turning often,
until onion and potatoes are
golden. Gently stir in celery, dill
pickle, and browned sausage.

Combine pickle liquid, sugar,
caraway seeds, and mustard;
pour over potato mixture. Cover,
reduce heat to low, and cook for
20 to 25 minutes or until potatoes
are tender when pierced; turn often. Season to taste with salt and
pepper. Garnish with parsley.
Makes 4 servings.

Almond Turkey & Peas

What's more convenient than an
easy supper that uses leftover
turkey or chicken? Our Oriental-
style, stovetop specialty combines cooked turkey, peas, snow
peas, sliced mushrooms, and
water chestnuts—all topped with
toasted slivered almonds. This
entrée cooks in less than 10 minutes and is great served over
steamed rice.

¼ cup slivered almonds
2 tablespoons butter or margarine
½ pound mushrooms, sliced
1 package (10 oz.) frozen peas
1 package (6 oz.) frozen snow
   peas
¾ cup chicken broth
½ cup sliced canned water
   chestnuts, drained
3 cups cooked turkey or chicken,
   cut in bite-size pieces
⅓ cup sliced green onions
   (including tops)
4 teaspoons cornstarch
1 tablespoon soy sauce
   About 4 cups steamed rice

Spread almonds in a shallow pan
and toast in a 300° oven until
lightly browned (about 8 minutes); set aside.

In a wide frying pan over
medium heat, melt butter. Add
mushrooms and cook until soft.
Add peas, snow peas, and ½ cup
of the broth. Cover and cook, stirring, for about 4 minutes or until
peas are thawed.

Stir in water chestnuts, turkey,
and onions; continue cooking and
stirring for about 2 more minutes.
Combine cornstarch, soy, and
remaining ¼ cup broth. Stir into
turkey mixture and cook until
sauce boils and thickens. Serve
over steamed rice and garnish
with almonds. Makes 4 to 6
servings.

Sweet & Sour Turkey Patties

Soy sauce and fresh ginger flavor
these miniature ground turkey
patties dotted with celery and
green onion. A fruity sweet and
sour sauce containing sliced
green pepper, carrots, and celery
is spooned over the patties just
before serving.

   Sweet and sour sauce (recipe
   follows)
1 egg
⅔ cup finely chopped celery
1 tablespoon *each* soy sauce and
   dry sherry
1 green onion (including top),
   finely chopped
2 cloves garlic, minced or pressed
1 teaspoon chopped fresh ginger
   or ¼ teaspoon ground ginger
2 teaspoons cornstarch
1 pound ground turkey
2 teaspoons butter or margarine
1 green pepper, seeded and cut
   into thin julienne strips
2 stalks celery, cut in ¼-inch
   slices
2 carrots, cut in ⅛-inch slices

Prepare sweet and sour sauce; set
aside.

Combine egg, chopped celery,
soy sauce, sherry, green onion,
garlic, ginger, and cornstarch.
Add turkey and mix well. Shape
into 12 patties, each about ½ inch
thick. (Mixture will be moist.)

In a wide frying pan over
medium heat, melt 1 teaspoon of
the butter. Add about half the
patties at a time and cook, turning carefully, until browned on
both sides (about 6 minutes *total*).
Remove from pan and set aside.

Melt remaining 1 teaspoon butter. Add green pepper, celery, and
carrots. Cook, stirring occasionally, for about 4 minutes, then remove from pan and set aside.

Return patties to pan and add
sweet and sour sauce. Cover, reduce heat, and simmer gently for
about 5 minutes. Transfer patties
to a warm serving platter. Return
vegetables to pan and cook for

about 2 minutes or until heated through, then spoon over patties. Makes 4 servings.

Sweet and sour sauce. Stir together ⅓ cup unsweetened **apple juice** or pineapple juice, 1 tablespoon **soy sauce**, 3 tablespoons **catsup**, 4 teaspoons **vinegar**, 1 clove **garlic** (minced or pressed), ½ teaspoon chopped **fresh ginger** or ⅛ teaspoon ground ginger, and a few drops **sesame oil** (optional).

Joe's Special

No one is sure of the exact origin of the one-dish meal called Joe's Special. Some say it goes back more than three generations and originated in a San Francisco restaurant.

Ground beef, onions, mushrooms, chopped spinach, and eggs combine in this easy-to-fix skillet dinner. You can vary the number of eggs to suit your taste, but the more you use, the more cohesive the mixture will be.

  2 **pounds lean ground beef**
  1 **tablespoon olive oil or salad oil**
  2 **medium-size onions, chopped**
  2 **cloves garlic, minced or pressed**
  ½ **pound mushrooms, sliced**
1¼ **teaspoons salt**
  ½ **teaspoon** *each* **ground nutmeg and oregano leaves**
  ¼ **teaspoon pepper**
  1 **package (10 oz.) frozen chopped spinach, thawed and drained well**
  ¼ **cup grated Parmesan cheese**
  4 **to 6 eggs, lightly beaten**
     Additional grated Parmesan cheese

In a wide frying pan over medium heat, cook beef in oil until crumbly and well browned. Add onions, garlic, and mushrooms; cook, stirring occasionally, until onions are soft.

Stir in salt, nutmeg, oregano, pepper, spinach, and cheese; cook for about 5 more minutes. Add eggs, reduce heat to low, and gently stir mixture until eggs are

set to your liking. Pass additional cheese at the table. Makes 4 to 6 servings.

Meatball-stuffed French Loaf

(Pictured on facing page)

Hearty meatballs of ground beef and pork, grated cheese, parsley, and bread crumbs are mounded high inside this unique, edible serving bowl—a hollowed-out, round loaf of French bread. Allow 3 or 4 meatballs per person, then cut the bread into wedges to serve.

1½ **pounds lean ground beef**
  ½ **pound lean ground pork**
  2 **eggs**
  ½ **cup** *each* **fine dry bread crumbs and grated Romano cheese**
  ¼ **cup chopped parsley**
  ½ **teaspoon salt**
  1 **package (1½ oz.) dry spaghetti-sauce mix with mushrooms**
  2 **tablespoons butter or margarine**
  1 **can (8 oz.) tomato sauce**
  ½ **cup water**
  1 **round loaf (about 2 lbs.) French bread**
     Additional chopped parsley (optional)
     Additional grated Romano cheese

Combine beef, pork, eggs, bread crumbs, the ½ cup cheese, the ¼ cup parsley, salt, and 2 tablespoons of the dry sauce mix. Shape into 20 to 24 meatballs, each about 1½ inches in diameter.

In a wide frying pan over medium heat, melt 1 tablespoon of the butter. Add half of the meatballs and cook, shaking pan to brown meatballs on all sides. Remove and set aside. Melt remaining 1 tablespoon butter and brown remaining meatballs. Remove from pan and set aside. Discard pan drippings, if necessary.

In same pan, blend remaining dry sauce mix with tomato sauce and water; heat until bubbly.

Return meatballs to pan. Cover, reduce heat, and simmer for about 25 minutes.

Meanwhile, cut off top third of the bread and scoop out insides (reserve for other uses), leaving a shell about 1 inch thick. Heat, uncovered, in a 350° oven for 10 minutes, if desired.

With a slotted spoon, transfer meatballs into warmed loaf. Garnish with parsley, if desired. Pour tomato sauce into a serving bowl to offer at the table. Pass additional grated cheese. Makes 6 to 8 servings.

Oriental Meatball Dinner

Bake these delicious ground beef and pork meatballs in advance, then complete the dish in a skillet for an easy, last-minute dinner.

  1 **pound lean ground beef**
1½ **pounds lean ground pork**
  1 **can (5 oz.) water chestnuts, drained and chopped**
  2 **eggs, beaten**
  ⅔ **cup quick-cooking rolled oats**
  ⅓ **cup chopped onion**
  1 **teaspoon ground ginger**
1½ **teaspoons salt**
  1 **can (14 oz.) beef broth**
  1 **tablespoon sesame seeds**
  2 **tablespoons salad oil**
  1 **medium-size green pepper, seeded and cut in julienne strips**
  3 **small zucchini, diagonally sliced**
  1 **medium-size onion, sliced**
  4 **stalks celery, diagonally sliced**
  4 **cloves garlic, minced or pressed**
  ⅔ **cup water**
  ¼ **cup soy sauce**
  3 **tablespoons cornstarch**
     About 4 cups hot cooked rice

(Continued on page 72)

Mounded high inside hollowed-out French bread, hearty parsley-cheese meatballs baked in tomato sauce highlight a fireside supper. Recipe is on this page.

In a large bowl, thoroughly combine beef, pork, water chestnuts, eggs, oats, chopped onion, ginger, salt, 2/3 cup of the broth, and sesame seeds. Using about 2 tablespoons of the mixture for each, shape into smooth balls.

Place meatballs slightly apart on ungreased, rimmed baking sheets. Bake in a 450° oven for 30 minutes or until meat is lightly browned. (At this point, you may cool, cover, and refrigerate until next day.)

Heat oil in a wide frying pan over medium heat; add green pepper, zucchini, sliced onion, celery, and garlic. Cook, stirring often, for about 4 minutes or until vegetables are tender-crisp.

Add meatballs (reheat first, if refrigerated), remaining broth, and water; bring to a simmer. Blend soy sauce with cornstarch; stir quickly into mixture and cook until sauce boils and thickens. Serve meatballs and sauce over rice. Makes 8 servings.

Orange-flavored Lamb Shanks

Both fresh orange juice and orange peel lend their subtle, fruity flavor to these tender, succulent lamb shanks. Hot fluffy rice and your favorite green or yellow vegetable would complete the menu.

    4   or 5 large oranges
 1½   teaspoons salt
  ½   teaspoon paprika
    6   lamb shanks (about 5 lbs.), with
        bones cracked
    2   tablespoons salad oil
    1   clove garlic, minced or pressed
    1   large onion, thinly sliced
  ½   teaspoon *each* ground allspice
        and cinnamon
    2   tablespoons cornstarch blended
        with 2 tablespoons water

Grate 2 teaspoons orange peel from 2 or 3 of the oranges. Ream 1 cup juice from the 2 or 3 oranges.

Remove and discard peel and white membrane from remaining oranges and cut oranges into thin, crosswise slices. Set aside.

Sprinkle salt and paprika over lamb. Heat oil in a 12 to 14-inch frying pan or 5 to 6-quart Dutch oven over medium heat. Add lamb shanks, a few at a time, and cook, turning, until well browned. Add garlic and onion; cook until soft.

Stir in orange peel, orange juice, allspice, and cinnamon. Bring to a boil. Cover, reduce heat, and simmer, turning meat occasionally, for 2 to 2½ hours or until lamb is very tender when pierced. With slotted spoon, transfer meat to a warm platter.

Skim off and discard fat from pan. Add cornstarch mixture and cook, stirring constantly, until mixture boils and thickens. Spoon over lamb. Garnish with orange slices. Makes 6 servings.

Herbed Lamb Shanks

The secret of this delicious lamb entrée is slow cooking. Brown the meaty shanks well, then let them simmer for at least two hours in a tasty, herb-flavored tomato and wine sauce.

    2   tablespoons salad oil
    4   lamb shanks (about 1 lb. *each*),
        with bones cracked
    2   cloves garlic, minced or pressed
    1   large onion, sliced
    1   large green pepper, seeded and
        thinly sliced
  ¾   teaspoon *each* thyme and savory
        leaves
    1   teaspoon salt
  ¼   teaspoon pepper
    1   can (12 oz.) tomato juice
  ½   cup dry red wine
    3   tablespoons all-purpose flour
        blended with 3 tablespoons
        water

Heat oil in a 12 to 14-inch frying pan or a 5-quart Dutch oven over medium heat. Add shanks, a few at a time, and cook until well browned. Remove from pan and set aside.

To the pan juices, add garlic, onion, and green pepper. Cook, stirring, until vegetables are soft. Stir in thyme, savory, salt, pepper, tomato juice, and wine; add lamb. Bring to a boil. Cover, reduce heat, and simmer for 2 to 2½ hours or until meat is very tender when pierced. (At this point you may cool, cover, and refrigerate until next day.)

Skim off and discard fat. (Reheat, if refrigerated.) Stir flour mixture into pan juices. Over medium heat, cook, stirring, until sauce boils and thickens. Makes 4 servings.

Lamb & Brown Rice Casserole

Lean, boneless lamb chunks, marinated in a tangy sauce, are browned and combined with mushrooms and brown rice. Just before serving, add currants for a sweet and surprising flavor.

 1½   pounds boneless lean lamb
  ¼   cup lemon juice
    3   tablespoons salad oil
    2   tablespoons firmly packed
        brown sugar
    1   clove garlic, minced or pressed
    1   tablespoon tomato-based chili
        sauce
  ½   teaspoon oregano leaves
    1   pound mushrooms, sliced
    1   cup brown rice
        Chicken broth
  ¼   cup currants

Remove and discard excess fat from lamb; cut lamb into ¾-inch cubes. Combine lemon juice, 2 tablespoons of the oil, sugar, garlic, chili sauce, and oregano; pour over meat. Cover and chill for 2 to 4 hours.

Heat remaining 1 tablespoon oil in a wide frying pan over medium heat. With a slotted spoon, lift meat from marinade (reserve marinade), drain briefly, and brown lamb in oil, a few pieces at a time. Remove lamb with a slotted spoon and set aside.

To the pan juices, add mushrooms and cook until soft. Stir in rice and lamb. To reserved marinade, add enough broth to make 2½ cups; stir into rice mixture. Cover, reduce heat, and simmer for about 1¼ hours or until lamb and rice are tender and liquid is absorbed. Just before serving, stir in currants. Makes 4 to 6 servings.

Stovetop Beef Stew

(Pictured on page 31)

Chunks of lean beef, small whole boiling potatoes, and large slices of carrot make a most satisfying hearty stew.

- ½ cup all-purpose flour
- 1 teaspoon *each* salt and sugar
- ½ teaspoon *each* pepper and paprika
- ¼ teaspoon ground cloves or allspice
- 2 pounds boneless lean beef, cut into 2-inch cubes
- 3 tablespoons salad oil
- 1 large onion, sliced
- 1 clove garlic, minced or pressed
- 2 whole bay leaves
- 1 teaspoon *each* lemon juice and Worcestershire
- 4 cups boiling water
- 6 to 8 small carrots
- 6 to 8 small boiling potatoes, center strip of peel removed

In a small bag, combine flour, salt, sugar, pepper, paprika, and cloves. Shake meat, a few pieces at a time, to coat completely.

Heat oil in a 12 to 14-inch frying pan or 5-quart Dutch oven over medium heat. Add meat and cook until well browned.

Add onion slices, garlic, and any extra flour mixture. Stir well; cook until bubbly. Add bay leaves, lemon juice, Worcestershire, and water; bring to a boil. Cover, reduce heat, and simmer for 1½ to 2 hours or until meat is tender when pierced. Stir in carrots and potatoes; cover and simmer for 20 to 25 more minutes or until vegetables are tender when pierced. Makes 6 servings.

Veal Stroganoff

Italian sausages give a spicy accent to this veal and vegetable combination; then sour cream is blended into the sherry-flavored sauce at the last minute. Hot cooked noodles or brown rice go well with this subtly seasoned skillet meal.

- 3 mild Italian sausages (about 3 oz. *each*), casings removed and cut in ½-inch slices
- 2 tablespoons salad oil
- 1½ pounds boneless veal, cut into 1½-inch cubes
- 1 medium-size onion, chopped
- ½ pound mushrooms, quartered
- 1 cup beef broth
- 1 medium-size red or green bell pepper, seeded and chopped
- ½ cup dry sherry (or additional beef broth)
- 1 cup sour cream
- 2 tablespoons all-purpose flour Salt, pepper, and ground nutmeg

Heat oil in a wide frying pan over medium-high heat. Add veal and sausages and cook, stirring occasionally, until well browned. Add onion and mushrooms and cook until onion is soft.

Stir in broth, bell pepper, and sherry. Bring to a boil. Cover, reduce heat, and simmer for about 1 hour or until meat is tender when pierced. Increase heat to high and cook, uncovered, until liquid is reduced to about 1 cup.

Combine sour cream and flour; gently stir into veal mixture until well blended and heated through. Season to taste with salt, pepper, and nutmeg. Makes 4 to 6 servings.

Skillet Stroganoff

This delicious version of beef Stroganoff is subtly flavored with Dijon mustard and nutmeg. Hot buttered noodles make a perfect accompaniment.

- 1½ pounds boneless lean beef Pepper
- 5 tablespoons butter or margarine
- 1 medium-size onion, finely chopped
- ½ pound mushrooms, thinly sliced
- 3 tablespoons all-purpose flour
- 1 cup beef broth
- 1 tablespoon Dijon mustard
- ¼ teaspoon freshly grated nutmeg or ground nutmeg
- ½ cup whipping cream Hot, cooked, buttered noodles Chopped parsley

Cut beef across grain in ¼-inch-thick slanting slices. Sprinkle meat generously with pepper.

In a wide frying pan over medium-high heat, melt 1 tablespoon of the butter. Add onion and cook, stirring occasionally, until soft. Add half the meat and cook, stirring, for about 5 minutes or until well browned. Remove from pan and set aside. Repeat, using 1 more tablespoon of the butter and remaining meat; remove from pan.

Over medium heat, melt remaining 3 tablespoons butter. Add mushrooms and cook, stirring, until soft. Blend in flour

(Continued on page 75)

and cook, stirring, until bubbly. Gradually pour in broth and continue cooking and stirring until sauce boils and thickens. Stir in mustard, meat-onion mixture, nutmeg, and cream; stir until heated through. Serve over noodles and garnish with parsley. Makes 4 to 6 servings.

Spinach-stuffed Chicken Breasts

Tucked inside each savory chicken breast is a stuffing of chopped spinach, bits of bacon and onion, seasoned croutons, and a hint of garlic. You make a pocket in the thick side of each boneless breast, fill it with the stuffing, and close it with a wooden pick.

- 8 slices bacon, diced
- 1 large onion, chopped
- 1 package (10 or 12 oz.) frozen chopped spinach, thawed and drained well
- 1 egg, lightly beaten
- ½ cup seasoned croutons, lightly crushed
- ½ teaspoon garlic salt
- 4 whole chicken breasts, split, skinned, and boned
  Salt and pepper
- 4 tablespoons butter, margarine, or salad oil
  Lemon wedges

In a wide frying pan over medium heat, cook bacon until crisp. Pour off all but 2 tablespoons of the drippings. Add onion and cook until soft.

With a slotted spoon, transfer bacon and onion to a large bowl. Add spinach, egg, croutons, and garlic salt; toss gently.

With a small sharp knife, cut a pocket in the thick side of each

---

Skillet version of classic chicken simmered in red wine (the French call it coq au vin) is ideal for entertaining, requiring little attention once assembled. Recipe is on this page.

breast half. Stuff lightly with spinach mixture and close with a wooden pick. (At this point you may cover and refrigerate until next day.)

Season lightly with salt and pepper. In same pan over medium heat, melt butter. Add chicken and cook, turning, for about 15 minutes (20 minutes, if refrigerated) or until meat in thickest portion is no longer pink when slashed. Serve with lemon wedges to squeeze over top. Makes 4 to 8 servings.

Classic Chicken with Wine

(Pictured on facing page)

In this traditional chicken dish, pork bits, onions, mushrooms, and pieces of chicken simmer together in red wine and beef broth. If you choose a varietal wine for the sauce, you can then name the dish after the wine, such as chicken Zinfandel or chicken Beaujolais.

- 1 pork shoulder chop (about ⅓ lb.), boned and cut into ½-inch cubes
- 1 broiler-fryer chicken (3 to 3½ lbs.), cut in pieces
- 8 to 10 small white onions, peeled
- ½ pound small mushrooms
- 1 can (14 oz.) beef broth
- 1 cup dry red wine
- 2 tablespoons *each* Dijon mustard and chopped parsley
- 1 teaspoon cornstarch blended with 1 teaspoon water

In a 12 to 14-inch frying pan or 5-quart Dutch oven over medium heat, cook pork in its own fat until well browned and crisp. Remove pork with a slotted spoon and set aside.

To the pan drippings, add chicken and onions. Cook, turning pieces occasionally, for about 20 minutes or until chicken and onions are well browned. Lift meat and vegetables from pan

and set aside. Stir in mushrooms and cook until soft; remove from pan and add to chicken.

Add broth to pan and bring to a boil, scraping brown pieces free from pan, until reduced to about 1 cup. Return chicken, onions, and mushrooms to pan. Add wine and mustard; bring to a boil. Cover, reduce heat, and simmer for about 30 minutes or until chicken thighs near bone are no longer pink when slashed. Stir in reserved pork and parsley; bring to a simmer again.

With a slotted spoon, lift meats and vegetables from pan and transfer to a warm serving platter. Stir cornstarch mixture into pan juices and quickly bring to a boil. Pour over chicken and vegetables. Makes 4 servings.

Biscuit-topped Chicken Ramekins

Topped with herb and cheese drop biscuits, these individual chicken and vegetable ramekins begin on the stovetop and finish in the oven. You can prepare the ramekins a day ahead, then add the drop biscuits just before slipping the casseroles into the oven to reheat.

- ½ pound bulk pork sausage
- 4 tablespoons butter or margarine
- 4 tablespoons all-purpose flour
- 1½ cups chicken broth
- 1 cup milk
- 2 cups shredded cooked chicken
- 2 packages (10 oz. *each*) frozen mixed vegetables, thawed, or 1 can (16 oz.) mixed vegetables, drained
  Salt and pepper
  Herb-cheese biscuits (recipe follows)

In a wide frying pan over medium heat, cook sausage until well browned. Remove from pan and drain on paper towels. Discard pan drippings.

(Continued on page 77)

Tips for freezing & transporting casseroles

A busy cook quickly learns the advantage of preparing casseroles ahead of time: wholesome entrées that are quickly ready, without last-minute kitchen chaos at dinnertime.

Prepared or partially prepared casseroles—with the exception of fish dishes—may be stored in the refrigerator for as long as 24 hours, before they're baked. Most of our recipes provide for this, and tell specifically the point at which a casserole may be refrigerated. They also give two different cooking times, since refrigerated dishes take slightly longer to bake.

Freezing

The trick to preserving natural flavors is to freeze food fast and keep it at 0°F or below. When foods freeze, the organisms that cause spoilage become inactive, so if casseroles stay solidly frozen, they can be kept in the freezer for 4 to 6 months.

Here are some tips for preparing and freezing entire casseroles or individual portions:

• Slightly undercook vegetables to prevent them from becoming mushy when defrosted.

• Omit potatoes from stew-type dishes.

• Use as little fat as possible—for example, in browning meat for a casserole.

• Cool casseroles rapidly by setting the dish in cold running water or in ice water.

• Line casserole dish with a piece of moisture-resistant paper (sometimes called freezer wrap) or aluminum foil large enough to wrap assembled casserole. Fill dish as recipe directs, seal to close, and freeze. Then remove dish. To bake, remove wrapping and return frozen casserole to dish.

• Avoid using foil when freezing casseroles with acidic ingredients such as tomatoes.

• Label frozen casseroles, identifying the type of food as well as the date. Check dates regularly to avoid storing longer than 4 to 6 months.

• Instead of baking when frozen, partially thaw casseroles at room temperature. This will help to prevent overcooking.

Here's an easy way to please fickle family members at mealtime. Try making a TV dinner at home by placing an individual serving of a casserole plus a helping of one or two favorite vegetable side dishes in a ramekin or other baking dish, or in a recycled aluminum dinner tray. Label it, perhaps including special information (such as "Brian's favorite lasagne without mushrooms"). Then wrap and freeze.

Transporting

Taking a casserole to someone else's house can be a problem, especially with a hot dish. If the distance is short and you simply want to keep the casserole hot, place it in a cloth-lined (old dish cloth or towel) or newspaper-lined cardboard carton and set it on a level place, such as the floor or trunk of your car.

For longer distances, you may want to consider partially baking your casserole at home, then finishing the baking at your destination. In either case, prevent spillage by not filling the dish to capacity.

You'll probably want to take garnishes with you to put on at just the right moment. And for the last word in potluck convenience, take along a trivet and serving utensil, too.

Melt butter in pan; blend in flour and cook until bubbly. Gradually pour in broth and milk and continue cooking until sauce boils and thickens. Stir in chicken, vegetable, and sausage. Season to taste with salt and pepper. Spoon mixture into 4 shallow ramekins, about 1½-cup size. (At this point you may cool, cover, and refrigerate until next day.)

Prepare herb-cheese biscuits. Spoon a quarter of the dough on each ramekin. Bake in a 400° oven for about 30 minutes (35 minutes, if refrigerated) or until bubbly and biscuits are well browned. Makes 4 servings.

Herb-cheese biscuits. Mix together 1 cup all-purpose **flour,** 1½ teaspoons **baking powder,** 4 tablespoons grated **Parmesan cheese,** and ½ teaspoon *each* **salt** and **celery seeds.** With a pastry blender or two knives, cut in 2 tablespoons **shortening.** Stir in ½ cup **milk** until well blended.

Chicken & Rice Pilaf

After the chicken is browned, it simmers on a bed of aromatic rice flavored with cinnamon, allspice, diced green pepper, and stewed tomatoes. You may use either a broiler-fryer cut in pieces or 6 legs with thighs attached.

- 2 tablespoons *each* **salad oil** and **butter**
- 1 **broiler-fryer chicken** (3 to 3½ lbs.), cut in pieces, or 6 legs with thighs
- 2 large **onions,** chopped
- 1 **green pepper,** seeded and diced
- 1 cup **brown** or **white rice**
  Hot water
- 3 **chicken bouillon cubes**
- ½ teaspoon **thyme leaves**
- ¼ teaspoon *each* **pepper,** ground **cinnamon,** and ground **allspice**
- 1½ teaspoons **salt**
- 1 can (8 oz.) **stewed tomatoes**
  Chopped parsley

Heat oil and butter in a 5 or 6-quart Dutch oven over medium heat. Add chicken pieces, a few at a time, and cook, turning occasionally, until well browned. Remove pieces and set aside.

Discard all but 4 tablespoons of the pan juices. Add onions and green pepper and cook for about 3 minutes or until onion is slightly soft. Stir in rice and cook for 5 more minutes.

Combine 2⅔ cups hot water (2 cups for white rice), bouillon cubes, thyme, pepper, cinnamon, allspice, and salt; pour over rice. Cover, reduce heat, and simmer for about 45 to 50 minutes (20 minutes for white rice) or until rice is almost tender.

Stir in tomatoes and arrange chicken pieces on top. Cover and simmer for about 25 more minutes or until meat near thigh bone is no longer pink when slashed and liquid is absorbed.

Arrange chicken pieces around rim of serving platter. Mound rice in center; sprinkle with parsley. Makes 4 to 6 servings.

Barbecued Pork with Brown Rice & Vegetables

(Pictured on page 79)

The Chinese have a delicious way of preparing barbecued pork in the oven. They use soy sauce, honey, sherry, ginger, and Chinese five-spice (a blend of ground cloves, fennel, licorice root, cinnamon, and star anise). We steep pork slices in a marinade made with the same ingredients, and barbecue the meat in the oven. Then we combine the pork with stir-fried vegetables and brown rice in this special skillet dinner. You can prepare the pork ahead of time and keep it refrigerated for as long as two days.

You'll need a 12 to 14-inch frying pan or wok. Have all the ingredients assembled close by, since actual cooking time is quite short.

- 2 to 3 cups **barbecued pork** (recipe follows)
- 2 tablespoons **salad oil**
- 2 medium-size **carrots,** thinly sliced
- 1 medium-size **onion,** thinly sliced
- 1 clove **garlic,** minced or pressed
- 1 large **green pepper,** seeded and cut into thin strips
- 2 small **zucchini,** thinly sliced
- ¼ pound **mushrooms,** thinly sliced
- 2 cups **bean sprouts**
- 1 to 2 cups **cold cooked brown rice**
- 4 to 6 tablespoons **soy sauce**
  Chopped fresh coriander (cilantro)

Prepare barbecued pork as directed; set aside 2 to 3 cups (reserve remaining pork for other uses).

Heat 1 tablespoon of the oil in a 12 to 14-inch frying pan or large wok over medium heat. Add carrots and cook for about 1 minute. Add onion, garlic, and green pepper; cook for about 1 minute, adding more oil as needed. Add

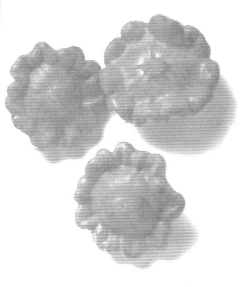

zucchini, mushrooms, and barbecued pork slices. Cook until all vegetables are just tender-crisp (about 2 minutes). Add bean sprouts and rice, stirring until heated through. Stir in soy sauce and sprinkle with coriander. Makes 4 to 6 servings.

Barbecued pork. In a pan over medium heat, combine ¼ cup **soy sauce;** 2 tablespoons *each* **honey, sugar,** and **dry sherry;** 1 teaspoon *each* **salt** and **Chinese five-spice;** and 3 quarter-size slices of **fresh ginger,** minced. Heat for 1 minute to dissolve sugar; let cool. Cut 3 pounds **boneless lean pork** into 1-inch-thick slices and place in a plastic bag. Pour cooled marinade over meat, then seal and refrigerate for 4 hours or until next day. Turn bag occasionally to distribute marinade.

Remove meat from marinade and place on a rack set over a foil-lined baking pan; reserve marinade. Bake in a 350° oven for 30 minutes. Turn pieces over and return to oven for 45 more minutes, brushing occasionally with reserved marinade. Cut slices into thin strips. Makes about 2½ pounds barbecued pork.

Finnan Haddie & Mushroom Casserole

Haddie, or finnan haddie, is smoked haddock (or even cod) fillets. Its unusual name is a variation of Findhorn haddock, a fish identified with Findhorn, the fishing port in Scotland where finnan haddie was first prepared.

Here is a creamy, nut-topped finnan haddie casserole. The fish fillets—either fresh or frozen—are poached in milk first, then cut into bite-size pieces and gently stirred into a savory cream sauce with mushrooms, Dijon mustard, and hard-cooked eggs. The traditional accompaniment for this casserole is boiled new potatoes.

About 1½ pounds finnan haddie (thawed, if frozen)
About 2 cups milk
3 tablespoons butter or margarine
¼ cup sliced almonds
½ pound mushrooms, sliced
3 tablespoons all-purpose flour
2 chicken bouillon cubes dissolved in 1 cup boiling water
¾ cup half-and-half (light cream)
½ teaspoon Dijon mustard
⅛ teaspoon liquid hot pepper seasoning
⅓ cup sliced green onion (including tops)
2 hard-cooked eggs, chopped
Salt and pepper
Boiled new potatoes (optional)

Place fish in a wide frying pan, cover with milk, and bring to a boil over medium heat. Cover, reduce heat, and simmer for 20 minutes or until fish flakes when prodded in thickest portion with a fork. Drain and discard milk. Break cooled fish into bite-size pieces; discard bones.

In a 3-quart pan over medium heat, melt butter. Add almonds and cook, stirring often, until golden. With a slotted spoon, remove from pan and set aside.

To the pan add mushrooms and cook until soft. Stir in flour and cook until bubbly. Gradually pour in bouillon and continue cooking and stirring until sauce boils and thickens. Stir in half-and-half, mustard, hot pepper seasoning, onion, eggs, and fish; mix well. Season to taste with salt and pepper. Turn into a serving dish. Garnish with almonds. Serve with boiled new potatoes, if desired. Makes 4 to 6 servings.

Fish Stew with Spicy Hot Mayonnaise

(Pictured on page 31)

The spicy hot mayonnaise adds creaminess and zest to this hearty fish casserole. You may choose any type of mild-flavored fish—rockfish, lingcod, haddock, or cod—for this entrée.

Spicy hot mayonnaise (recipe follows)
2 tablespoons salad oil
1 large onion, chopped
1 large green pepper, seeded and chopped
2 cloves garlic, minced or pressed
1 can (16 oz.) pear-shaped tomatoes
1½ cups water
½ cup dry white wine
1 bottle (8 oz.) clam juice
3 chicken bouillon cubes
¼ teaspoon *each* basil, oregano, and thyme leaves
2 pounds boneless, lean, mild-flavored fish fillets (suggestions above)
Salt and pepper
Chopped parsley

Prepare spicy hot mayonnaise.

Heat oil in a 12 to 14-inch frying pan or 5-quart Dutch oven over medium heat. Add onion, pepper, and garlic; cook until vegetables are soft. Stir in tomatoes (break up with a spoon) and their liquid, water, wine, clam juice, bouillon cubes, basil, oregano, and thyme. Bring to a boil. Cover, reduce heat, and simmer for 15 minutes. (At this point you may cool, cover, and refrigerate until next day.)

Cut fish fillets into 1-inch cubes. Bring broth to a boil again. Add fish, cover, reduce heat, and simmer for 6 to 8 minutes or until fish flakes when prodded with fork. Season to taste with salt and pepper. Sprinkle with parsley. Pass spicy hot mayonnaise to stir into individual servings. Makes 4 to 6 servings.

Spicy hot mayonnaise. Combine ⅔ cup **mayonnaise,** 2 cloves minced or pressed **garlic,** ¾ to 1 teaspoon **cayenne,** 1 tablespoon **white wine vinegar,** and ¼ teaspoon **salt.** Cover and refrigerate, if made ahead.

Oriental stovetop specialty combines slivers of barbecued pork, tender-crisp vegetables, and brown rice in soy-flavored sauce. Recipe is on page 77.

SUPER SIDE DISHES

Vegetables & rice highlight these casseroles

Asparagus Parmesan

Bright green pieces of fresh asparagus bake in a smooth, curry-flavored cheese sauce in less than half an hour. Like so many vegetable casseroles, this one can be prepared the day before, ready to reheat just before dinner.

2½ pounds asparagus
    Boiling salted water
¼ cup butter or margarine
3 tablespoons chopped green onions (including tops)
⅓ cup all-purpose flour
¼ teaspoon curry powder
½ teaspoon salt
1½ cups milk
½ cup dry white wine
⅓ cup grated Parmesan cheese

Snap off tough ends of asparagus and cut stalks into 1-inch-long diagonal slices. Cook in boiling salted water (or steam over boiling water) until tender-crisp; drain.

In a pan over medium-high heat, melt butter. Add onions and cook until soft. Blend in flour, curry powder, and salt and cook, stirring, until bubbly. Gradually pour in milk and wine and continue cooking and stirring until sauce boils and thickens.

Add asparagus pieces and turn mixture into a shallow 1½-quart casserole or 9-inch-square baking dish. Sprinkle with cheese. (At this point you may cover and refrigerate until next day.)

Bake, uncovered, in a 400° oven for 15 to 20 minutes (30 minutes, if refrigerated) or until heated through. Makes about 4 servings.

Green Beans Supreme

Just four ingredients—green beans, canned soup, oregano, and French-fried onions—combine to make this popular vegetable side dish.

2 packages (9 oz. *each*) frozen green beans, cooked and drained
2 cups (about 1½ cans) condensed cream of mushroom soup
½ teaspoon oregano leaves
1 can (3½ oz.) French-fried onions

Combine beans, soup, and oregano. Turn into a shallow 1½-quart casserole or 9-inch-square baking dish. (At this point, you

may cover and refrigerate until next day.)

Bake, uncovered, in a 350° oven for 20 minutes (30 minutes, if refrigerated). Sprinkle top evenly with onions and return to oven for 5 more minutes or until heated through. Makes about 6 servings.

Green Beans in Swiss Cheese Sauce

Fresh green beans and sliced mushrooms combine in an herb-cheese sauce seasoned with a little dry sherry. You can prepare this dish ahead, then reheat it just before serving.

1½ pounds green beans
    Boiling salted water
¼ cup butter or margarine
1 small onion, chopped
½ pound mushrooms, sliced
3 tablespoons all-purpose flour
1 teaspoon salt
⅛ teaspoon *each* pepper, thyme leaves, and marjoram leaves
1 cup milk
1 cup (about 4 oz.) shredded Swiss cheese
⅓ cup dry sherry or milk

Break off ends and cut beans into 2-inch lengths. Cook in boiling salted water (or steam over boiling water) until tender-crisp (about 5 minutes); drain immediately and set aside.

In a wide frying pan over medium heat, melt butter. Add onion and mushrooms and cook until soft. Blend in flour, salt, pepper, thyme, and marjoram and cook, stirring, until bubbly. Gradually pour in milk and continue cooking and stirring until sauce boils and thickens.

Remove from heat and blend in 1/2 cup of the cheese as well as sherry. Stir in beans and turn into a shallow 1 1/2-quart casserole or 9-inch-square baking dish. Sprinkle top with remaining 1/2 cup cheese. (At this point you may cover and refrigerate until next day.)

Bake, uncovered, in a 400° oven for about 30 minutes (40 minutes, if refrigerated) or until heated through. Makes about 6 servings.

Green Beans Oriental

There's lots of crunch in this Oriental-style vegetable casserole featuring green beans, bean sprouts, water chestnuts, and French fried onions. All bake together in a smooth sauce made with mushroom soup.

2 packages (9 oz. *each*) frozen French-cut green beans
  Boiling salted water
2 tablespoons butter or margarine
2 tablespoons minced onion
1 1/2 cups bean sprouts
1 can (8 oz.) water chestnuts, drained and sliced
  Butter or margarine
1 can (10 3/4 oz.) condensed cream of mushroom soup
1/2 soup can milk
1/2 cup shredded sharp Cheddar cheese
1 can (3 1/2 oz.) French-fried onions

Cook beans in boiling salted water according to package directions; drain and set aside.

In a wide frying pan over medium heat, melt butter. Add onion, bean sprouts, and water chestnuts; cover pan and cook for 3 to 4 minutes.

Spread half the beans in a buttered shallow 2-quart casserole or 7 by 11-inch baking dish. Cover with half the sprout mixture. Combine soup and milk; spoon half of it over vegetables. Repeat layers, using remaining beans, sprout mixture, and soup. Sprinkle top with cheese. (At this point, you may cover and refrigerate until next day.)

Bake, uncovered, in a 400° oven for about 25 minutes (35 minutes, if refrigerated). Distribute onions evenly over top and return to oven for 5 more minutes or until bubbly and heated through. Makes about 8 servings.

Chile Bean Bake

Here is a filling chile bean dish to serve with Mexican food when you want a change from the traditional refried beans.

2 cans (15 oz. *each*) pinto beans, drained
1 can (15 oz.) chile with beans
1 can (8 oz.) bean dip with jalapeños
1 green pepper, seeded and chopped
1/2 cup minced green onions (including tops)
2 tablespoons tomato-based chile sauce
1 cup (about 4 oz.) shredded Cheddar cheese

In a large bowl, combine pinto beans, chile, bean dip, green pepper, green onions, and chile sauce. Blend well and turn into a shallow 2-quart casserole or 7 by 11-inch baking dish. Sprinkle with cheese. (At this point you may cover and refrigerate until next day.)

Bake, uncovered, in a 325° oven for 45 minutes or until heated through. (If refrigerated, bake, covered, for 30 minutes; then uncover and bake for 25 more minutes.) Makes about 6 servings.

Rum-baked Beans

For an unusual variation on the ordinary baked bean dish, try this casserole featuring thick-sliced bacon, pineapple, strong coffee, and dark rum.

1/2 pound thick-sliced bacon
4 cans (1 lb. 3 oz. *each*) baked beans
2 teaspoons dry mustard
1/4 teaspoon ground ginger
1/4 cup strong coffee
1/2 cup firmly packed dark brown sugar
1/2 cup dark rum
1 can (8 1/4 oz.) sliced pineapple, drained

(Continued on next page)

Cut bacon into 2-inch lengths. In a wide frying pan over medium heat, cook bacon until crisp; drain and set aside.

Combine beans, mustard, ginger, coffee, brown sugar, and bacon. Turn into a 3-quart casserole or 9 by 13-inch baking dish. (At this point you may cover and refrigerate until next day.)

Bake, covered, in a 350° oven for 45 minutes. Stir in rum. Cut pineapple slices in half and arrange over top. Return to oven, uncovered, for about 25 more minutes or until top is browned. Makes 10 to 12 servings.

Cheesy Baked Limas

Bacon, Swiss cheese, and seasoned croutons offer a delicious medley of flavors when combined with baby limas.

- 6 strips bacon, diced
- 1 small onion, chopped
- 1 small green pepper, seeded and chopped
- 1 teaspoon dry basil
- 2 tablespoons all-purpose flour
- ¾ cup chicken broth
- 2 cups (about 8 oz.) shredded Swiss or Cheddar cheese
- 2 packages (10 oz. *each*) frozen baby limas, thawed
- ¾ cup seasoned croutons

In a wide frying pan over medium heat, cook bacon until crisp; remove bacon and discard all but 2 tablespoons drippings.

To drippings, add onion and green pepper and cook, stirring, until vegetables are soft. Blend in basil and flour and cook, stirring, until bubbly. Gradually pour in broth and continue cooking and stirring until sauce boils and thickens.

Add cheese, stirring just until melted. Add limas and bacon. Turn mixture into a shallow 1½-quart casserole or 9-inch-square baking dish. (At this point you

may cover and refrigerate until next day.)

Sprinkle with croutons and bake, uncovered, in a 350° oven for about 20 minutes (35 to 40 minutes, if refrigerated) or until bubbly and heated through. Makes 4 to 6 servings.

Broccoli & Rice Casserole

Chopped broccoli and cooked rice combine in this easy, make-ahead vegetable casserole. The zesty cheese sauce is made with canned soup and a jar of processed cheese spread.

- 3 packages (10 oz. *each*) frozen chopped broccoli
- 3 cups cold cooked rice
- 2 tablespoons butter or margarine
- 1 large onion, chopped
- 1 cup chopped celery
- 1 can (10¾ oz.) condensed cream of chicken soup
- 1 jar (8 oz.) pasteurized process cheese spread
- ¼ teaspoon ground nutmeg
- ½ cup *each* milk and chopped almonds

Place broccoli in a colander; thaw and drain well. Combine broccoli and rice and turn into a shallow 3-quart casserole or 9 by 13-inch baking dish.

In a wide frying pan over medium heat, melt butter. Add onion and celery and cook, stirring, until vegetables are soft. Add soup, cheese spread, nutmeg, and milk. Continue cooking and stirring until sauce is smoothly blended. Pour sauce over broccoli-rice mixture and stir gently to mix. (At this point you may cover and refrigerate until next day.)

Bake, covered, in a 350° oven for about 25 minutes (45 minutes, if refrigerated). Remove cover, sprinkle with nuts, and return to oven for 15 more minutes. Makes about 6 servings.

Coriander Broccoli & Carrots

A creamy coriander-flavored white sauce seasoned with Dijon mustard coats steamed chunks of carrots and broccoli.

- 1 pound *each* broccoli and carrots Boiling water
- 4 tablespoons butter or margarine
- 1 small onion, chopped
- 3 tablespoons all-purpose flour
- 1 teaspoon ground coriander
- ⅛ teaspoon *each* ground nutmeg and pepper
- ½ teaspoon salt
- 1 teaspoon chicken stock base dissolved in 1 cup hot water
- ½ cup half-and-half (light cream)
- 1½ teaspoons Dijon mustard
- 3 tablespoons minced parsley

Peel broccoli stems and carrots; cut flowerets from broccoli and set aside. Cut broccoli stems and carrots into ½-inch pieces and steam over boiling water for about 8 minutes. Add broccoli flowerets and continue steaming for 3 more minutes. Plunge vegetables into cold water; drain.

In a wide frying pan over medium heat, melt butter. Add onion and cook until soft. Blend in flour, coriander, nutmeg, pepper, and salt and cook, stirring, until bubbly. Gradually pour in chicken stock and half-and-half and continue cooking and stirring until sauce boils and thickens. Stir in mustard, parsley, carrots, and broccoli.

Turn mixture into a shallow 2-quart casserole or 7 by 11-inch baking dish. (At this point you may cover and refrigerate until next day.)

Bake, uncovered, in a 375° oven for 25 to 35 minutes (40 to 45 minutes, if refrigerated) or until heated. Makes about 6 servings.

Carrot Soufflé

Light and airy, this colorful soufflé goes together quickly for a festive, last-minute side dish. The ingredients—eggs, shredded carrots, minced chives, and skim milk (rather than cream)—make this dish low in calories.

> **About 2 tablespoons butter or margarine**
> 2 **cups packed shredded carrots**
> 3 **tablespoons water**
> 1 **teaspoon salt**
> 1 **tablespoon minced chives**
> 4 **tablespoons all-purpose flour**
> 1 **cup skim milk**
> 4 **eggs, separated**

Preheat oven to 375°.

Generously butter bottom and sides of a 1½ or 2-quart soufflé dish or casserole; set aside.

In a wide frying pan over medium heat, melt 1 tablespoon of the butter. Add carrots, water, salt, and chives. Cover and cook, stirring occasionally, until carrots are tender (about 5 minutes).

Blend in flour and cook, stirring, until bubbly. Gradually pour in milk and continue cooking and stirring until sauce boils and thickens. Add egg yolks, beating vigorously with a fork.

Whip egg whites until soft, moist peaks form; carefully fold egg whites into carrot mixture. Pour into prepared soufflé dish.

Bake in preheated 375° oven for about 35 minutes or until puffed and lightly browned. Serve immediately. Makes 4 to 6 servings.

Carrot & Rice Casserole

The unusual flavor of this rice casserole comes from grated orange peel, ginger, and chopped parsley.

> ¾ **cup uncooked rice**
> **Butter or margarine**
> 1½ **cups thinly sliced carrots**
> ¼ **teaspoon** *each* **ground ginger and grated orange peel**
> 1 **tablespoon** *each* **chopped parsley and instant minced onion**
> 2 **teaspoons chicken stock base dissolved in 1½ cups boiling water**
> 1 **tablespoon butter or margarine**

Place rice in a shallow pan; brown lightly in a 400° oven for 8 to 10 minutes. Turn rice into a lightly buttered shallow 1½-quart casserole or 8-inch-square baking dish. Stir in carrots, ginger, orange peel, parsley, and onion. Combine chicken stock with butter; when butter is melted, pour stock over rice.

Bake, covered, in a 400° oven for 20 to 25 minutes or until liquid has been absorbed. Makes about 4 servings.

Gingered Carrots

Diagonally sliced carrots seasoned with brown sugar and finely chopped crystallized ginger are an excellent side dish for roast pork or ham.

> 1 **teaspoon olive oil**
> 4 **cups diagonally sliced carrots, cut ⅛ inch thick**
> 1 **cup water**
> ⅛ **teaspoon garlic powder**
> 1 **tablespoon** *each* **brown sugar and finely chopped crystalized or preserved ginger**
> 2 **tablespoons white wine vinegar**
> ¼ **teaspoon salt**
> 2 **teaspoons chopped parsley**

Heat oil in a wide frying pan over medium heat. Add carrots, water, garlic powder, brown sugar, ginger, vinegar, and salt. Cook, covered, until carrots are tender-crisp (8 to 10 minutes). Sprinkle with parsley to serve. Makes about 6 servings.

Baked Corn with Tomato-Cheese Topping

Thin slices of tomato sprinkled with Parmesan cheese cover a spicy corn and green pepper mixture seasoned with prepared salad dressing. This is a colorful side dish for Mexican food and goes well with a cooling salad and icy cold beer.

> **About 6 to 7 ears uncooked corn**
> 3 **green onions (including tops), sliced**
> 1 **small green pepper, seeded and diced**
> 2 **tablespoons prepared green goddess salad dressing**
> ¼ **cup sour cream or unflavored yogurt**
> 1 **teaspoon brown sugar**
> 1 **tablespoon all-purpose flour**
> ¼ **teaspoon salt**
> ⅛ **teaspoon pepper**
> 1 **tablespoon butter or margarine**
> 1 **large tomato, sliced**
> ¼ **cup grated Parmesan cheese**

Using a sharp knife and leaving rough kernel bases attached to cob, cut raw corn kernels from cob to make 3 cups. Place in a shallow 1½-quart casserole or 9-inch-square baking dish. Scatter onions and green pepper over corn.

Combine salad dressing, sour cream, brown sugar, flour, salt, and pepper. Spoon mixture over vegetables; dot with butter.

Bake, covered, in a 375° oven for 35 minutes. Stir well. Arrange tomato slices on top, and sprinkle evenly with cheese. Return to oven, uncovered, for 10 more minutes. Makes about 6 servings.

Herbed Mushrooms

Sliced mushrooms flavored with green pepper, celery, mustard, lemon juice, and Worcestershire are the perfect accompaniment for grilled meats or cold cuts.

- 1 tablespoon *each* lemon juice, prepared mustard, and Worcestershire
- ⅔ cup water
- ¾ teaspoon *each* thyme and marjoram leaves
- 3 tablespoons butter or margarine
- 1½ pounds mushrooms, sliced
- 1 medium-size onion, chopped
- ½ cup *each* chopped green pepper and celery
- 1 clove garlic, minced or pressed
- 1 tablespoon all-purpose flour
- Salt and pepper

In a small bowl, combine lemon juice, mustard, Worcestershire, water, thyme, and marjoram; set aside.

In a wide frying pan over medium-high heat, melt 2 tablespoons of the butter. Add mushrooms and cook, stirring, until golden; lift out and set aside. In pan, melt remaining 1 tablespoon butter. Add onion, green pepper, celery, and garlic and cook, stirring, until soft. Blend in flour and cook, stirring, until bubbly. Gradually pour in lemon juice mixture and continue cooking and stirring until sauce boils and thickens. Add mushrooms and season to taste with salt and pepper. Makes about 6 servings.

Baked Marinated Onions

Thick slices of onion, marinated in a zesty combination of oil, vinegar, and lots of seasonings, bake slowly in the oven until tender. You can save any leftover marinade to use as a salad dressing; cover and refrigerate up to 2 weeks.

- 3 large onions
- ¾ cup salad oil
- ⅓ cup white wine vinegar
- ½ teaspoon *each* dry basil, thyme leaves, and oregano leaves
- ¼ teaspoon *each* sugar and salt
- ⅛ teaspoon pepper
- Paprika
- Chopped parsley

Peel onions and cut into ½-inch-thick slices. Arrange slices in a single layer in a shallow 3-quart casserole or 9 by 13-inch baking dish.

In a small jar or bowl, combine oil, vinegar, basil, thyme, oregano, sugar, salt, and pepper; shake or stir to blend thoroughly. Pour marinade over onions and let stand at room temperature for 1 to 2 hours. (At this point you may cover and refrigerate until next day.)

Pour off and reserve marinade. Bake onions, covered, in a 350° oven for about 30 minutes. Uncover, baste lightly with reserved marinade, sprinkle with paprika, and bake, uncovered, for 30 more minutes or until onions are tender when pierced. Garnish with parsley. Makes about 6 servings.

Potato Salad Casserole

Similar to hot potato salad, this casserole combines sliced cooked potatoes with green pepper, onion, and crumbled bacon.

- 8 strips bacon
- 1 small onion, finely chopped
- ⅓ cup wine vinegar
- 1 teaspoon salt
- ¼ teaspoon pepper
- 4 teaspoons sugar
- 2 pounds thin-skinned potatoes, cooked and peeled
- ½ green pepper, seeded and finely chopped

In a wide frying pan over medium heat, cook bacon until crisp. Remove from pan, reserving drippings; drain and set aside.

To pan drippings, add onion, vinegar, salt, pepper, and sugar. Cook, uncovered, for about 3 minutes.

Slice potatoes into a shallow 1½-quart casserole or 8-inch-square baking dish. Crumble bacon and scatter over potatoes along with green pepper. Pour in hot dressing and mix together lightly.

Bake, uncovered, in a 375° oven for about 20 minutes. Serve hot. Makes about 6 servings.

Potatoes au Gratin

A rich, creamy sauce, made with Swiss cheese and whipping cream and seasoned with nutmeg and a hint of garlic, covers thin slices of potatoes. Long, slow baking produces the brown, slightly crunchy crust.

- 2 pounds russet or thin-skinned potatoes
- ¼ cup butter or margarine, softened
- 3 cloves garlic, minced or pressed
- 2½ cups (about 10 oz.) shredded Swiss cheese
- 1 small onion, chopped
- Salt, pepper, and ground nutmeg
- 2 eggs
- 2 cups whipping cream or half-and-half (light cream)

Peel potatoes and cover with cold water. Cut potatoes into thin slices; return slices to cold water.

Combine 2 tablespoons of the butter with a third of the minced garlic; rub mixture on bottom and sides of a shallow 2-quart casserole or 7 by 11-inch baking dish.

Drain potato slices on paper towels; pat dry. Arrange a quarter of the slices in an overlapping layer in pan. Toss 2 cups of the cheese with onion and remaining minced garlic. Spoon a quarter of this mixture over potatoes, then sprinkle with salt, pepper, and nutmeg. Repeat layering with potatoes, cheese mixture, and seasonings 3 more times.

Beat together eggs and whipping cream; spoon over potatoes. Sprinkle with remaining ½ cup cheese and dot with remaining butter.

Bake, uncovered, in a 350° oven for 1¼ hours or until top is browned and potatoes are tender when pierced. Makes 4 to 6 servings.

Potatoes Anna

Paper-thin slices of russet potatoes are layered with melted butter and grated Parmesan cheese in this classic French recipe. Our potato cake bakes to a crisp, brown outside and a creamy, soft inside.

    About 2½ pounds russet
        potatoes
    ½ cup melted butter or margarine
    ½ cup grated Parmesan cheese
        Salt and pepper

Peel potatoes and cover with cold water. Cut potatoes into paper-thin (about ⅛-inch) slices; return slices to cold water.

Grease a 9-inch cake pan (one with a nonstick finish is preferable) or a shallow 2-quart casserole. Drizzle bottom of pan with 1 tablespoon of the butter.

Drain potato slices on paper towels; pat dry. Arrange a sixth of the slices in an overlapping

layer in pan. Drizzle potatoes with another 1 tablespoon of the butter; lightly sprinkle with some of the Parmesan cheese, salt, and pepper. Repeat layering with potatoes, butter, cheese, and seasonings; drizzle top with any remaining butter. With a heavy pan, press down potatoes to compress them.

Bake, covered, in a 425° oven for about 30 minutes. Uncover and bake for 35 to 45 more minutes or until potatoes are browned and crisp on top and around edges. Let stand for 5 minutes.

With a large spatula, hold potatoes in place and drain off excess butter. Loosen potatoes around edges and invert on a serving platter. Makes about 6 servings.

Rocky Mountain Raclette

Inspired by the classic Swiss dish, raclette, we have combined baked potatoes with onion, chiles, bacon, and cheese. Just before serving, you broil the potato halves in the oven.

    4 medium-size russet potatoes
    1 large, mild white onion, sliced
    ½ cup prepared Italian salad
        dressing
    4 tablespoons butter or margarine
    1 can (4 oz.) diced green chiles,
        drained
    10 strips bacon, crisply cooked,
        drained, and crumbled
    1½ cups (about 6 oz.) shredded
        Swiss cheese

Scrub potatoes well; pat dry. With a fork, prick skin in several places. Bake in a 400° oven for about 1 hour (or in a microwave oven on full power for about 15 minutes) or until potatoes are soft when squeezed.

Meanwhile, place onion slices in a bowl. Pour salad dressing over onions and set aside at room temperature.

Split cooked potatoes lengthwise and place on a rimmed baking sheet. With a fork, lightly mash each potato half in its skin and mix in butter and chiles. Spoon onion slices and dressing evenly over each, then sprinkle each with bacon and cheese. Broil 4 to 6 inches from heat for about 2 minutes or just until cheese begins to melt. Makes 8 servings.

Browned Potato Loaf

For something a little out of the ordinary, try serving this crusty, oven-browned potato dish. Combine cooked potatoes, minced parsley, heated milk, butter, and flour until stiff; then press the mixture into a loaf pan. After refrigerating for several hours, the loaf is turned out onto a platter, sprinkled with cheese, and cooked in the oven until golden brown and crusty.

    3 tablespoons *each* butter or
        margarine and all-purpose
        flour
    1 cup milk
    4 or 5 medium-size russet
        potatoes, cooked, peeled, and
        diced or thinly sliced
    1 tablespoon minced parsley
    1 teaspoon salt
    ¼ teaspoon pepper
    ¾ cup shredded sharp Cheddar
        cheese
        Parsley sprigs

In a pan over medium heat, melt butter. Blend in flour and cook, stirring, until bubbly. Gradually pour in milk and continue cooking and stirring until sauce boils and thickens. Stir in potatoes and parsley. Reduce heat to low and cook, stirring occasionally, until mixture is fairly stiff (about 5 minutes). Sprinkle with salt and pepper.

Turn into a well-greased 5 by 9-inch loaf pan, press down firmly, and refrigerate for several hours or until next day.

(Continued on page 88)

Casserole breads
...the container's the thing

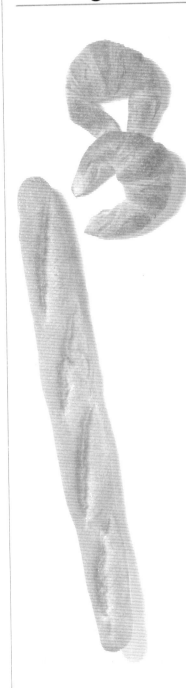

Herb Corn Bread

Just as casseroles can be baked, served, and stored in their original dishes, so can this savory corn bread. Coffee cans give this moist bread its distinctive shape—tall, round, and domed.

The plastic lids that come with the cans prove useful, too, at several different stages. They seal the batter in the can for freezing if you want to bake the bread another time. They also tell you when the dough (which rises only once) is ready to bake—they pop off. And once a baked loaf is sliced below the top of the can, the lid will seal in the bread to keep it fresh.

A variation for raisin-nut bread, also baked in coffee cans, is given as well.

- 1 package active dry yeast
- ½ cup warm water (about 110°)
- 2 teaspoons celery seeds
- 3 tablespoons sugar
- 1½ teaspoons ground sage
- ⅛ teaspoon *each* ground ginger and ground marjoram
- 1 large can (13 oz.) evaporated milk
- 1 teaspoon salt
- 2 tablespoons salad oil
- ½ cup yellow cornmeal
- 3½ to 4 cups all-purpose flour, unsifted
  Butter or margarine, softened

In a large bowl, dissolve yeast in water; blend in celery seeds, 1 tablespoon of the sugar, sage, ginger, and marjoram. Let stand in a warm place until bubbly (about 15 minutes). Stir in remaining 2 tablespoons sugar, along with milk, salt, and oil. Gradually beat in cornmeal and enough of the flour, 1 cup at a time, to make batter very heavy and stiff, but too sticky to knead.

Divide batter in half and spoon into 2 well-greased 1-pound cans or spoon all the batter into a well-greased 2-pound coffee can. Cover with greased plastic can lids. (At this point you may freeze.)

Let covered cans stand in a warm place until batter rises and pops off plastic lids (45 to 55 minutes for 1-pound cans, 55 to 60 minutes for 2-pound can).

If frozen, let batter stand in covered cans at room temperature until lids pop (4 to 5 hours for 1-pound cans, 6 to 8 hours for 2-pound can).

Bake, uncovered, in a 350° oven for about 45 minutes for 1-pound cans, about 1 hour for 2-pound can; crust will be very brown. Brush tops lightly with butter. Let cool in cans on a rack for 10 minutes. With a thin knife, loosen crust around edge of can, slide bread from can, and let bread continue to cool in an upright position on rack. Makes 2 small loaves or 1 large loaf.

Raisin-nut bread. Follow instructions for corn bread, but omit celery seeds, sage, marjoram, and cornmeal. Instead, add 1 teaspoon **ground cinnamon** and ½ teaspoon **ground nutmeg** to the yeast mixture. Stir ½ cup *each* **raisins** and **chopped walnuts** into batter with final addition of flour.

Cheese & Dill Bread

Here's a quick, no-knead method for making a Parmesan-flavored batter bread seasoned with a sprinkling of dill seeds. You can bake the bread in two 2-quart casseroles or soufflé dishes or in one large 4 or 5-quart dish. You might also want to try the variation for cheddar-caraway bread that follows.

- 1 large can (13 oz.) evaporated milk
- 3 tablespoons *each* sugar and instant minced onion
- 3 tablespoons butter or margarine, cut into pieces
- 2 teaspoons salt
- 1 tablespoon dill seeds
- 1 cup (3 oz.) grated Parmesan cheese
- 1 package active dry yeast
- ¼ cup warm water (about 110°)
- 3¾ cups all-purpose flour, unsifted
- 2 eggs

In a pan, combine milk, sugar, onion, butter, salt, dill seeds, and cheese. Heat, stirring, to about 110° (butter and cheese do not need to melt completely).

In a large bowl, dissolve yeast in water. Add warm milk mixture; beat in 1½ cups of the flour. Add eggs, one at a time, beating well after each addition. Gradually beat in another 1½ cups flour until batter is smooth. With a spoon, beat in remaining ¾ cup flour. Cover and let rise in a warm place until doubled (about 45 minutes).

Stir batter down and spoon into 2 generously greased 2-quart casseroles or soufflé dishes (or one 4 or 5-quart dish or 10-inch tube pan). Cover and let rise in a warm place until almost doubled (about 45 minutes).

Bake in a 350° oven for 40 to 45 minutes for 2 loaves (55 minutes for 1 large loaf) or until bread sounds hollow when tapped. Let cool in casserole on a rack for 10 minutes; then let bread continue to cool in an upright position on rack. Makes 2 small loaves or 1 large loaf.

Cheddar-caraway bread. Follow instructions for making cheese and dill bread, but omit minced onion, dill seeds, and grated cheese. Instead, add 1½ cups (6 oz.) shredded sharp **Cheddar cheese,** 2 teaspoons **caraway seeds,** and ½ teaspoon **garlic powder** to the milk mixture.

Three Wheat Batter Bread

(Pictured on page 18)

Hearty, nutritious ingredients— wheat germ, cracked wheat, and whole wheat flour—go into this easy batter bread. Instead of using a 2-quart casserole, try baking the bread in either two 1-pound coffee cans or one 2-pound can. (See recipe for herb corn bread, page 86.)

1 package active dry yeast
½ cup warm water (about 110°)
⅛ teaspoon ground ginger
3 tablespoons honey
1 large can (13 oz.) evaporated milk
1 teaspoon salt
2 tablespoons salad oil
2½ cups all-purpose flour, unsifted
1¼ cups whole wheat flour, unsifted
½ cup wheat germ
¼ cup cracked wheat

In a large bowl, combine yeast, water, ginger, and 1 tablespoon of the honey; let stand in a warm place until bubbly (about 20 minutes). Stir in remaining 2 tablespoons honey, milk, salt, and oil. Stir together all-purpose flour, whole wheat flour, wheat germ, and cracked wheat; add 1 cup at a time to liquid ingredients, beating well after each addition.

Divide batter in half and spoon into 2 well-greased 1-pound coffee cans or spoon all the batter into a well-greased 2-pound coffee can. Cover with greased plastic can lids. (At this point you may freeze.)

Let covered cans stand in a warm place until batter rises and pops off plastic lids (55 to 60 minutes for 1-pound cans, 1 to 1½ hours for 2-pound can).

If frozen, let batter stand in covered cans at room temperature until lids pop (4 to 5 hours for 1-pound cans, 6 to 8 hours for 2-pound can).

Bake, uncovered, in a 350° oven for about 45 minutes for 1-pound cans, about 1 hour for 2-pound can, or until bread sounds hollow when tapped. Let cool in cans on a rack for 10 minutes. With a thin knife, loosen crust around edge of can, slide bread from can, and let bread continue to cool in an upright position on rack. Makes 2 small loaves or 1 large loaf.

Caraway Potato Bread

With this recipe, you'll get two large, round loaves of delicious potato bread flavored with caraway seeds, minced onion, and bacon bits.

½ cup warm water (about 110°)
2 packages active dry yeast
3 tablespoons sugar
2 cups mashed potatoes
4 tablespoons butter or margarine, softened
1 large can (13 oz.) evaporated milk
½ cup imitation bacon bits
2 tablespoons instant minced onion
1 tablespoon caraway seeds
2 teaspoons garlic salt
1 teaspoon salt
2 eggs
About 6½ cups all-purpose flour, unsifted

In a small bowl, combine water, yeast, and sugar; let stand until foamy (about 10 minutes).

Place mashed potatoes in a large bowl. Beat in butter; then gradually beat in evaporated milk until blended. Add bacon bits, onion, caraway seeds, garlic salt, salt, eggs, yeast mixture, and 3 cups of the flour; beat until thoroughly blended.

Gradually stir in 2 to 2½ more cups of the flour. Turn dough out on a heavily floured board. Knead dough until smooth and elastic (about 10 minutes), adding remaining flour to board as necessary to prevent sticking.

Place dough in a greased bowl, turning to grease top; cover and let rise in a warm place until doubled (about 1½ to 2 hours).

Punch dough down and knead briefly to release air. Divide dough in half. Shape each half into a round and place each round in a greased 2-quart casserole or soufflé dish. Cover and let rise in a warm place until almost doubled (about 40 minutes).

Bake, uncovered, in a 350° oven for 40 to 45 minutes or until loaves are richly browned on top and sound hollow when tapped. Turn loaves out onto a wire rack to cool. Makes 2 round loaves.

About half an hour before serving, turn loaf out onto an oven-proof platter or baking sheet. Sprinkle with cheese. Bake, uncovered, in a 375° oven for 30 to 40 minutes or until golden brown. Garnish with parsley sprigs. Makes about 6 servings.

Pea & Celery Medley

Peas and celery are layered with a mixture of mushrooms, water chestnuts, and canned soup in this long-time favorite casserole. We used cream of mushroom soup, but any can of condensed cream soup may be substituted.

- 2 **tablespoons butter or margarine**
- 2 **cups diagonally sliced celery, cut ½ inch thick**
- 3 **tablespoons water**
- 2 **packages (10 oz. *each*) frozen peas**
- 1 **can (10¾ oz.) condensed cream of mushroom soup**
- 1 **can (3 or 4 oz.) sliced mushrooms**
- 1 **can (5 oz.) water chestnuts, drained and sliced**
- 1 **tablespoon butter, melted**
- ¾ **cup fresh bread crumbs**

In a wide frying pan over medium heat, melt the 2 tablespoons butter. Add celery and water; cover and cook, stirring occasionally, until celery is tender-crisp (about 4 minutes). Add peas and continue cooking for 5 more minutes.

Combine soup, mushrooms and their liquid, and water chestnuts. Arrange half the vegetables in bottom of a greased shallow 1½-quart casserole or 8-inch-square baking dish and cover with half the soup mixture. Repeat layering. (At this point, you may cover and refrigerate until next day.)

Combine the 1 tablespoon melted butter and bread crumbs; sprinkle over top. Bake, uncovered, in a 350° oven for about 20 minutes (30 minutes, if refrigerated) or until bubbly. Makes 4 to 6 servings.

Savory Sauerkraut

Just five additional ingredients are needed to spice up a jar of prepared sauerkraut. Try serving this savory side dish with grilled frankfurters or other cooked sausages and a glass of cold beer.

- 3 **tablespoons bacon drippings or butter or margarine**
- 1 **medium-size onion, chopped**
- 1 **jar (1 lb.) sauerkraut, drained**
- 1 **can (1 lb.) tomatoes**
- ½ **teaspoon *each* caraway seeds and sugar**

In a wide frying pan over medium heat, melt bacon drippings. Add onion and cook until soft. Stir in sauerkraut, tomatoes (break up with a spoon) and their liquid, caraway seeds, and sugar; mix thoroughly. Turn into a 1-quart casserole or 8-inch-square baking dish. (At this point, you may cover and refrigerate until next day.)

Bake, uncovered, in a 350° oven for about 30 minutes (40 minutes, if refrigerated) or until heated through. Makes 4 to 6 servings.

Spinach & Artichokes au Gratin

Colorful layers of marinated artichoke hearts and chopped spinach are covered with a smooth cream cheese sauce, then baked until lightly browned.

- 2 **jars (6 oz. *each*) marinated artichoke hearts**
- 3 **packages (10 oz. *each*) frozen chopped spinach, thawed**
- 3 **packages (3 oz. *each*) cream cheese**
- 4 **tablespoons butter or margarine, softened**
- 6 **tablespoons milk Pepper**
- ⅓ **cup grated Parmesan cheese**

Drain marinade from artichokes, saving marinade for other uses. Reserving a few for garnish, distribute remaining artichokes over the bottom of a shallow 1½-quart casserole or 9-inch-square baking dish.

Squeeze out as much moisture as possible from spinach and arrange evenly over artichokes. With a mixer, beat cream cheese and butter until smooth and fluffy; gradually blend in milk. Spread mixture over spinach, sprinkle lightly with pepper, then dust with Parmesan cheese. (At this point you may cover and refrigerate until next day.)

Bake, uncovered, in a 375° oven for 40 minutes (50 minutes, if refrigerated) or until top is lightly browned. Garnish with reserved artichokes. Makes about 6 servings.

Spinach & Artichoke Custard Squares

A thick custard featuring chopped spinach and marinated artichoke hearts bakes under a layer of two kinds of cheese.

2 packages (10 oz. *each*) frozen
  chopped spinach, thawed
1 jar (6 oz.) marinated artichoke
  hearts
2 tablespoons butter or
  margarine
1 medium-size onion, chopped
¼ teaspoon ground nutmeg
¾ teaspoon oregano leaves
1 can (10¾ oz.) condensed cream
  of celery soup
4 eggs, lightly beaten
⅛ teaspoon pepper
1 large package (8 oz.) cream
  cheese, softened
⅓ cup *each* milk and grated
  Parmesan cheese

Squeeze out as much moisture as
possible from spinach; set aside.

Drain artichokes, reserving 2
tablespoons of the marinade; then
chop artichokes.

Heat reserved marinade with
butter in a wide frying pan over
medium heat. Add onion and
cook, stirring, until soft. Stir in
spinach, artichokes, nutmeg,
oregano, soup, eggs, and pepper.
Spoon mixture into a greased
shallow 1½-quart casserole or
9-inch-square baking dish; gently
smooth top with a knife. Beat
together cream cheese, milk, and
Parmesan cheese until smooth.
Spread evenly over spinach
mixture.

Bake, uncovered, in a 325°
oven for about 35 minutes or until
center feels firm when lightly
pressed. Makes about 6 servings.

Curried Squash Bake

Layer three varieties of squash, a
curry-flavored sauce, wheat
germ, and two kinds of cheese;
then bake this substantial side
dish and serve it with grilled lamb
or pork.

2 *each* medium-size zucchini,
  crookneck, and patty pan
  squash (about 1½ lbs. *total*)
½ cup mayonnaise
2 teaspoons *each* prepared
  mustard and Worcestershire
1 teaspoon *each* curry powder and
  dry mustard
½ teaspoon ground ginger
¼ cup *each* toasted wheat germ
  and grated Parmesan cheese
2 cups (about 8 oz.) shredded jack
  cheese

Cut squash into ¼-inch slices and
steam over boiling water until
tender-crisp (about 5 minutes).

Combine mayonnaise, pre-
pared mustard, Worcestershire,
curry powder, dry mustard, and
ginger. Place half the squash in
the bottom of a greased shallow
2-quart casserole or 7 by 11-inch
baking dish. Top with half the
mayonnaise mixture, half the
wheat germ, half the Parmesan
cheese, and half the jack cheese.
Repeat layers. (At this point you
may cover and refrigerate until
next day.)

Bake, covered, in a 375° oven
for about 20 minutes (30 minutes,
if refrigerated) or until mixture is
bubbly and cheese is melted.
Makes 4 to 6 servings.

Zucchini-stuffed Tomatoes

For those summer months when
tomatoes and zucchini are in good
supply both in the markets and in
your garden, try these plump tomatoes filled with finely chopped
zucchini and green pepper. They
make a tasty, colorful addition to
any meal.

6 medium-size tomatoes
2 tablespoons salad oil
1 small onion, chopped
1 small green pepper, seeded and
  chopped
1 pound zucchini, finely chopped
1 clove garlic, minced or pressed
¾ teaspoon *each* oregano leaves
  and dry basil
½ teaspoon salt
¼ teaspoon pepper
2 eggs, lightly beaten
4 tablespoons grated Parmesan
  cheese

Peel tomatoes, if desired, then
cut out cores, seeds, and some of
the pulp. Drain tomato shells
upside-down.

Heat oil in a wide frying pan
over medium-high heat. Add
onion and green pepper and cook
until onion is soft. Stir in zucchini,
garlic, oregano, basil, salt, and
pepper. Continue cooking and
stirring for about 5 minutes. Stir
in eggs and 2 tablespoons of the
cheese. Spoon zucchini mixture
evenly into tomato shells; sprinkle
tops with remaining Parmesan
cheese.

Bake, uncovered, in a 350° oven
for 15 minutes or until heated
through. Makes 6 servings.

Tomato-Garlic Zucchini Bake

Slices of zucchini and onion are
quickly sautéed, then combined
with tomato wedges, Swiss
cheese, and sourdough bread
crumbs in this Italian-style side
dish.

4 tablespoons butter or margarine
1 small onion, coarsely chopped
3 medium-size zucchini, sliced
  ¼ inch thick
3 cloves garlic, minced or pressed
3 large tomatoes, peeled and cut
  into wedges
1⅓ cup (5⅓ oz.) diced Swiss cheese
1 cup sourdough bread crumbs
  Salt and pepper
2 teaspoons dry basil

(Continued on next page)

In a wide frying pan over medium heat, melt butter. Add onion, zucchini, and garlic and cook until soft. Add tomatoes, 1 cup of the cheese, and ¾ cup of the bread crumbs; toss gently. Season to taste with salt and pepper; stir in basil. Pour into a shallow 1½-quart casserole or 9-inch-square baking dish. Top with remaining ⅓ cup cheese and ¼ cup bread crumbs.

Bake, uncovered, in a 375° oven for 30 minutes or until bubbly. Makes 4 to 6 servings.

crisp (about 8 minutes); place in a colander to cool.

In a large bowl, combine soup, yogurt, cheese, salt, black pepper, and red pepper. Add zucchini and carrot-onion mixture and mix well. Spoon into a shallow 3-quart casserole or 9 by 13-inch baking dish. Combine bread crumbs and melted butter; sprinkle evenly over mixture. (At this point, you may cover and refrigerate until next day.)

Bake, uncovered, in a 350° oven for about 40 minutes (50 minutes, if refrigerated) or until bubbly and heated through. Makes 6 to 8 servings.

more sugar or salt, if necessary. Mix in 2 tablespoons of the butter. Spoon into a 1-quart casserole or soufflé dish. (At this point, you may cover and refrigerate until next day.)

In a small frying pan over medium heat, melt remaining 1 tablespoon butter. Add cashews and cook, stirring, until lightly toasted. Sprinkle over casserole.

Bake, uncovered, in a 375° oven for about 15 minutes (35 minutes, if refrigerated) or until heated through. Makes about 4 servings.

Crunchy Zucchini & Carrots

Slices of zucchini and carrots bake in a mild sauce made with canned soup, unflavored yogurt, and Cheddar cheese. Top the casserole with bread crumbs for a slightly browned appearance and a subtle crunch.

- 4 tablespoons butter or margarine
- 1 medium-size onion, chopped
- 8 medium-size (about 1 lb.) carrots, peeled and cut into ¼-inch slices
- 5 medium-size (about 2 lbs.) zucchini, cut into ¾-inch-thick slices
- 1 can (10¾ oz.) condensed cream of chicken or cream of mushroom soup
- ½ cup unflavored yogurt
- 1 cup (about 4 oz.) shredded Cheddar cheese
- ¼ teaspoon *each* each salt and pepper
  Dash of ground red pepper (cayenne)
- ¼ cup dry bread crumbs
- 2 tablespoons melted butter

In a wide frying pan over medium-high heat, melt butter. Add onion and carrots and cook, stirring, until carrots are tender when pierced (about 10 minutes). Remove from heat and cool briefly.

Meanwhile, steam zucchini over boiling water until tender-

Yam & Cashew Casserole

Yams or sweet potatoes are cooked until tender, then mashed and combined with cashews and seasonings in this unusually delicious side dish. A perfect accompaniment for your holiday baked ham or roasted turkey, this casserole can be doubled or even tripled for a large crowd.

- 2½ pounds yams or sweet potatoes
  Boiling salted water
- 1 teaspoon ground cinnamon
- ¼ teaspoon salt
- 1 egg
  About ¼ cup *each* pineapple juice or apple juice
- ¼ cup sugar
- 3 tablespoons butter or margarine, melted
- ½ cup salted cashews, coarsely chopped

Cook yams in boiling salted water until tender when pierced (about 30 minutes). Drain well; when cool enough to handle, peel.

Using an electric mixer, beat yams until mashed (you should have about 3 cups). Stir in cinnamon, salt, egg, juice, and sugar; continue beating until mixture is fluffy, adding more fruit juice if mixture seems dry. Taste, and add

Classic Pilaf

Pilaf is simply long grain white rice that is lightly browned in butter along with onion and garlic, then cooked until tender in broth —either chicken or beef. It is often tossed with a small amount of grated cheese just before serving. Though pilaf can be baked in the oven, it's easier to let it simmer on the stove.

- 4 tablespoons butter or margarine
- 1 medium-size onion, chopped
- 1 clove garlic, minced or pressed
- 1 cup rice
- 2 cups chicken or beef broth
  Salt
- ¼ cup grated Parmesan cheese (optional)

In a wide frying pan over medium heat, melt butter. Add onion and garlic and cook until onion is soft. Stir in rice and continue cooking, stirring occasionally, until rice is lightly browned.

Pour in chicken broth and bring to a boil. Cover, reduce heat, and simmer until rice is tender to bite (about 25 minutes). Stir once or twice and season to taste with salt. Toss gently with cheese, if desired. Makes about 4 servings.

Mixed Grain Pilaf

Here's a savory mixture of three types of grain—barley, brown rice, and bulgur wheat—plus vegetables and nuts, all combining to make a slightly chewy pilaf.

- ¼ cup butter or margarine
- ⅓ cup chopped almonds or walnuts
- 1 large onion, chopped
- 1 large carrot, chopped or shredded
- 1 clove garlic, minced or pressed
- ⅓ cup chopped parsley
- ⅓ cup *each* barley, brown rice, and bulgur (cracked wheat)
- 2½ cups beef or chicken broth
- ¼ cup dry sherry or water
- ¾ teaspoon *each* dry basil and oregano leaves
  Salt and pepper

In a 3-quart pan over medium heat, melt butter. Add nuts and stir until lightly toasted; with a slotted spoon, remove nuts and set aside.

Raise heat to medium-high and add onion, carrot, garlic, and parsley. Cook, stirring, until vegetables are soft. Add barley, rice, and bulgur; continue cooking and stirring until grains are lightly browned. Stir in broth, sherry, basil, and oregano; bring to a boil. Cover, reduce heat, and simmer until tender (about 45 minutes).

Remove pan from heat and let stand, covered, for about 10 min-

utes. Add salt and pepper to taste. Garnish with toasted nuts. Makes about 6 servings.

Cracked Wheat Vegetable Pilaf

Baked in an herb-tomato sauce, bulgur wheat's natural nutty flavor blends beautifully with a variety of vegetables in this easy pilaf.

- 1 cup bulgur (cracked wheat)
- 1 cup chicken, beef, or vegetable broth (or water)
- 2 tablespoons chopped parsley
- ¼ cup diced green or red bell pepper or carrot
- ½ cup thinly sliced green onions (including tops)
- 2 cups (about 8 oz.) finely diced Cheddar, Swiss, or jack cheese
- 1 cup whole kernel corn, cut off the cob, or frozen and thawed
- 1 egg, lightly beaten
- 1 can (8 oz.) tomato sauce
- 1 teaspoon dry basil
- ½ teaspoon *each* oregano leaves and garlic salt
- ¼ teaspoon pepper

In a bowl, combine bulgur and broth; stirring occasionally, let stand until liquid is absorbed (about 1 hour). Stir in parsley, green pepper, onions, cheese, corn, and egg.

Combine tomato sauce, basil, oregano, garlic salt, and pepper. Stir into bulgur mixture and mix well. Spoon into a greased shallow 2-quart casserole or 7 by 11-inch baking dish. (At this point you may cover and refrigerate until next day.)

Bake, covered, in a 350° oven for about 25 minutes (35 minutes, if refrigerated) or until bulgur is tender and mixture is heated through. Makes about 6 servings.

Risotto

Risotto is rice cooked to a creamy, flowing consistency. Even in its plainest form, seasoned only with a little onion, garlic, broth, and cheese, risotto is distinctive and worthy of presentation as a side dish for roasted or grilled meat.

- 2 tablespoons *each* butter and olive oil
- 1 medium-size onion, chopped
- 1 clove garlic, minced or pressed
- 1 cup rice
  About 3½ cups chicken broth
  Salt
- ½ cup grated Parmesan, Asiago, or Romano cheese
- 1 tablespoon butter or margarine
  Grated Parmesan, Asiago, or Romano cheese (optional)

Heat the 2 tablespoons butter and olive oil in a heavy 2-quart pan (or frying pan with a lid) over medium heat. Add onion and cook until soft. Stir in garlic and rice; continue cooking and stirring until rice is opaque (about 3 minutes).

Add 1 cup of the broth; bring to a boil. Cover, reduce heat, and simmer until liquid has been absorbed (about 10 minutes). Add remaining 2½ cups broth in 2 or 3 additions, removing cover each time and stirring lightly with a fork. Continue cooking until rice is tender and most of the liquid has been absorbed (about 20 to 25 more minutes). Season to taste with salt.

Remove pan from heat and add ¼ cup of the cheese and the 1 tablespoon butter; mix lightly with two forks. Turn into a serving dish and top with remaining ¼ cup cheese. Pass cheese at the table, if desired. Makes 4 to 6 servings.

Confetti Rice

You create this unusual dish simply by stirring chopped raw vegetables and almonds into cooking rice 10 minutes before it's done. We used green onions, carrots, and celery, but you can use broccoli, asparagus, or any other vegetables.

  4 tablespoons butter or margarine
1¼ cups rice
  1 cup *each* chicken or beef broth and water
  ½ teaspoon salt
  ¼ teaspoon dry basil
  ¾ cup *each* finely chopped carrots, celery, and green onions (including tops)
  ¼ cup sliced almonds
    Chopped parsley

In a large frying pan over medium heat, melt butter. Add rice and cook, stirring occasionally, until heated through but not browned (about 5 minutes). Stir in broth, water, salt, and basil; bring to a boil. Turn mixture into a 1½ or 2-quart casserole or soufflé dish.

Bake, covered, in a 375° oven for about 20 minutes or until rice is almost tender and most of the liquid is absorbed. Remove from oven and carefully stir in carrots, celery, green onions, and almonds. Cover and return to oven for about 10 more minutes or until rice is tender to bite and liquid is absorbed. (Vegetables should be crisp.) Sprinkle with chopped parsley. Makes about 6 servings.

Cumin Rice with Pine Nuts

Here's a colorful, nut-studded rice casserole that makes a delicious accompaniment for chicken, lamb, or turkey.

  5 tablespoons butter or margarine
1½ cups rice
1½ teaspoons salt
  1 tablespoon ground cumin
  3 cups boiling water
  ½ cup pine nuts or slivered almonds
    Parsley sprig

In a wide frying pan over medium heat, melt 2 tablespoons of the butter. Add rice and cook, stirring, until lightly browned. Stir in salt, cumin, and boiling water; bring to a boil. Cover, reduce heat, and simmer until rice is tender to bite and liquid is absorbed (about 25 minutes).

Meanwhile, in a pan over medium heat, melt remaining 3 tablespoons butter. Stir in pine nuts and cook, shaking pan often, until nuts are browned to your liking. Spoon over hot rice. Garnish with parsley. Makes about 6 servings.

The addition of fresh minced parsley, onion, and mild Cheddar cheese transforms simply cooked rice into something quite special.

  1 cup cold cooked rice
  1 cup (4 oz.) shredded mild Cheddar cheese
  1 egg, beaten
  ½ cup finely chopped parsley
  4 tablespoons butter or margarine, melted
  ¾ cup milk
  1 small onion, finely chopped

In a large bowl, combine rice, cheese, egg, parsley, butter, milk, and onion. Turn into a lightly greased 2-quart casserole or soufflé dish. (At this point you may cover and refrigerate until next day.)

Bake, uncovered, in a 350° oven for about 40 to 45 minutes (55 to 60 minutes, if refrigerated) or until set and top is lightly browned. Makes about 6 servings.

Green Vegetable Rice

In this festive casserole, the vegetables—spinach, parsley, and green onion—give flavor as well as color to the rice. If you have a food processor, you can chop the vegetables in minutes.

  3 to 4 cups cooked rice
  ¼ cup butter or margarine, softened
  2 teaspoons lemon juice
  ½ cup slivered or sliced almonds
  1 clove garlic, minced or pressed
  1 medium-size onion, chopped
  ½ teaspoon salt
  2 cups firmly packed, finely chopped spinach (about ¾ lb.)
  ½ cup *each* chopped green onions (including tops) and finely minced parsley
  1 egg
  1 cup milk

In a large bowl, combine rice, butter, lemon juice, nuts, garlic, onion, salt, spinach, green onions, and parsley.

Beat together egg and milk and add to rice mixture; toss gently. Turn into a greased shallow 3-quart casserole or 9 by 13-inch baking dish. (At this point, you may cover and refrigerate until next day.)

Bake, uncovered, in a 350° oven for 30 minutes (about 50 minutes, if refrigerated) or until custard is set. Stir lightly to serve. Makes 4 to 6 servings.

Mexican Rice with Tomatoes

Sliced avocado and wedges of tomato garnish this colorful, spicy rice dish flavored with ripe olives, green pepper, and just the right amount of Mexican seasonings. It's especially good served with barbecued meats.

- 3 to 4 cups cooked rice
- 1 can (2¼ oz.) sliced ripe olives, drained
- 1 small green pepper, seeded and chopped
    Butter or margarine
- 1 tablespoon butter or margarine
- 1 small onion, chopped
- ¾ cup beef broth
- 1½ teaspoons chili powder
- ¼ teaspoon *each* ground cinnamon, ground cumin, and oregano leaves
- ½ teaspoon salt
- 1 avocado
- 2 tablespoons lemon juice
- 2 medium-size tomatoes, cut in wedges

Combine rice, olives, and green pepper; turn into a buttered 1½ or 2-quart casserole.

In a wide frying pan over medium heat, melt the 1 tablespoon butter. Add onion and cook until soft. Stir in broth, chili powder, cinnamon, cumin, oregano, and salt. Reduce heat and simmer,

uncovered, for about 5 minutes; pour over rice mixture.

Bake, covered, in a 375° oven for about 25 minutes or until heated through.

Meanwhile, peel, pit, and slice avocado; sprinkle with 1 tablespoon of the lemon juice.

Stir remaining 1 tablespoon lemon juice into casserole. Garnish with avocado slices and tomato wedges. Makes about 6 servings.

Barley Vegetable Casserole

Start this easy vegetable casserole 1½ hours before dinner and let it cook in the oven. To make an easy meal of it, serve with broiled ground lamb patties and a crisp green salad tossed with orange segments.

- ¼ cup butter or margarine
- 1 pound mushrooms, sliced
- ¾ cup pearl barley
- 1 can (10¾ oz.) condensed cream of onion soup
- 2 cups water
- 2 packages (10 oz. *each*) frozen mixed vegetables, thawed

In a wide frying pan over medium heat, melt butter. Add mushrooms and cook, stirring, until soft. Add barley and continue cooking and stirring until mushroom liquid is absorbed. Stir in soup and water; blend well. Transfer mixture to a shallow 3-quart casserole or 9 by 13-inch baking dish.

Bake, covered, in a 350° oven for about 1 hour. Stir in mixed vegetables; cover and return to oven for 20 more minutes or until barley is tender. Fluff with a fork before serving. Makes 4 to 6 servings.

Spicy Lentils in Tomato Sauce

Protein-packed lentils simmer in a spicy tomato sauce studded with finely chopped bacon. Serve with grilled ham or barbecued frankfurters, or as a main dish with whole wheat bread and a fruit salad.

- 1 package (12 oz.) lentils
- 1 teaspoon salt
    About 3 cups water
- 4 strips bacon, finely diced
- 2 cans (8 oz. *each*) tomato sauce
- 1 medium-size onion, finely chopped
- ¼ cup firmly packed brown sugar
- 2 tablespoons prepared mustard
- ⅓ cup molasses

Rinse lentils; sort through and discard any foreign material. Drain well. Place in a 2½ or 3-quart casserole with a lid. Add salt, 3 cups water, bacon, tomato sauce, onion, brown sugar, mustard, and molasses; stir well.

Bake, covered, in a 350° oven for about 2 hours, stirring gently every 30 minutes. Add a little more water if sauce becomes too thick. Lentils are cooked when they mash readily and when liquid is bubbly and thickened. Makes about 6 servings.

Index

Almond turkey & peas, 69
Arroz con pollo, 44
Artichoke, chicken & mushroom casserole, 12
Artichoke & cheese custard squares, 35
Artichoke & chicken crêpes, 56
Artichoke & fila chicken casserole, 11
Artichoke & olive soufflé, 33
Artichoke & spinach custard squares, 88
Artichoke hearts & chicken, 62
Artichokes & spinach au gratin, 88
Artichoke-zucchini, filling, for deep-dish pizzas, 41
Asparagus, with cheese-topped chicken, 16
Asparagus Parmesan, 80

Bacon & vegetables, with piperade, 68
Baked chicken paprika, 19
Baked chiles rellenos, 45
Baked cod with capers, 27
Baked corn with tomato-cheese topping, 83
Baked kotleti, 51
Baked lentils with cheese, 43
Baked marinated onions, 84
Baked turkey legs & vegetables, 64
Barbecued pork, for brown rice & vegetables, 78
Barbecued pork with brown rice & vegetables, 77
Barley & chicken casserole, 29
Barley vegetable casserole, 93
Basic crêpes, 56
Bean & beef enchiladas, 44
Bean & beef stew, hearty, 4
Bean bake, chile, 81
Beans, green, in Swiss cheese sauce, 80
Beans, green, Oriental, 81
Beans, green, supreme, 80
Beans, lima, cheesy baked, 82
Beans, rum-baked, 81
Beef
baked kotleti, 51
& bean stew, hearty, 4
boeuf bourguignon, 54
corned, & cabbage, 52
corned, hash casserole, 9
curry, ground, 68
fiesta tamale pie, 45
Hungarian goulash, 53
Joe's special, 70
& kidney pie, English, 52
lasagne belmonte, 51
meatball dinner, Oriental, 70
meatball-stuffed French loaf, 70
meatballs with yogurt sauce, Greek, 60

Beef, (cont'd.)
moussaka Dubrovnik, 48
& mushrooms, biscuit-topped, 5
oven short ribs with noodles, 6
pastitsio, 48
pot au feu, 59
stew, savory, 4
stew, stovetop, 73
Stroganoff, skillet, 73
Stroganoff with poppy seed noodles, 53
& vegetable casserole, Sicilian, 5
Yorkshire relleno, 6
See also Beef recipes listed by title below
Beef & bean enchiladas, 44
Beef cabbage rolls with sauerkraut, 6
Beef Stroganoff with poppy seed noodles, 53
Beef tongue creole, 10
Biscuit-topped beef & mushrooms, 5
Biscuit-topped chicken ramekins, 75
Boeuf bourguignon, 54
Breads, casserole, 86-87
Broccoli & carrots, coriander, 82
Broccoli & chicken Mornay, 13
Broccoli & rice casserole, 82
Broccoli soufflé with cheese sauce, 35
Browned potato loaf, 85
Brown rice, ham & spinach, 9
Brown rice & lamb casserole, 72
Brown rice & vegetables, with barbecued pork, 77
Brown rice-vegetable casserole with salsa, 36
Buttered mushrooms, for spinach onion crêpes, 57
Buttery pastry, for crab & onion pie, 30

Cabbage & corned beef, 52
Cabbage rolls, beef, with sauerkraut, 6
Cacciatore, chicken, 49
Camembert soufflé, 33
Capers, with baked cod, 27
Caraway-Cheddar bread, 87
Caraway potato bread, 87
Carrot & rice casserole, 83
Carrots & broccoli, coriander, 82
Carrots & potatoes, with chicken, 19
Carrots & zucchini, crunchy, 90
Carrots, gingered, 83
Carrots, with orange chicken, 61
Carrot soufflé, 83
Cashew & yam casserole, 90
Casserole breads, 86-87
Celery & pea medley, 88

Celery root & fish ramekins, 22
Chard, Swiss, & cheese pie, 40
Chard, Swiss, with rice & cheese stuffing, 37
Cheddar-caraway bread, 87
Cheddar cheese sauce, for broccoli soufflé, 35
Cheese, with baked lentils, 43
Cheese & artichoke custard squares, 35
Cheese & dill bread, 86
Cheese & macaroni, red hot, 37
Cheese & mushroom manicotti, 37
Cheese & rice stuffing, with Swiss chard, 37
Cheese & sausage-stuffed pasta, 7
Cheese & Swiss chard pie, 40
Cheese-crusted mushroom soufflé, 33
Cheese enchiladas, stacked, 32
Cheese parsley rice, 92
Cheese pie, ratatouille, 38
Cheese sauce, Cheddar, for broccoli soufflé, 35
Cheese sauce, Swiss, green beans in, 80
Cheese-topped chicken with asparagus, 16
Cheese-topped fish fillets, 64
Cheesy baked limas, 82
Chicken
arroz con pollo, 44
& artichoke casserole, fila, 11
with asparagus, cheese-topped, 16
breasts, crab-stuffed, 16
breasts, spinach-stuffed, 75
breasts in orange sauce, 13
with carrots, orange, 61
cassoulet, 54
& corn pie, Chilean, 21
& dumplings, 17
lemon, 62
Mexican baked, 20
Oriental, 62
oven-sautéed garlic, 20
paella, 46
paprika, baked, 19
& peaches, spiced, 20
pie, lattice-topped, 12
ramekins, biscuit-topped, 75
sesame, in tarragon cream, 19
tarragon, 13
& tortillas, layered chile, 11
in white wine, savory, 17
with wine, classic, 75
See also Chicken recipes listed by title below
Chicken, mushroom & artichoke casserole, 12
Chicken & artichoke crêpes, 56
Chicken & artichoke hearts, 62
Chicken & barley casserole, 29
Chicken & broccoli Mornay, 13

Chicken & dumplings, 17
Chicken & rice pilaf, 77
Chicken & vegetables in wine, 61
Chicken breasts in orange sauce, 13
Chicken cacciatore, 49
Chicken cream enchiladas, 45
Chicken Dijon, 16
Chicken Tetrazzini, 49
Chicken with potatoes & carrots, 19
Chile, green, strata & sausage, 8
Chilean corn & chicken pie, 21
Chile & egg puff, 35
Chile bean bake, 81
Chile chicken & tortillas, layered, 11
Chile corn pie with fresh tomato salsa, 43
Chiles rellenos, baked, 45
Classic chicken with wine, 75
Classic pilaf, 90
Cod with capers, baked, 27
Confetti rice, 92
Coquilles St. Jacques, 59
Coriander broccoli & carrots, 82
Corn & chicken pie, Chilean, 21
Corn bread, herb, 86
Corned beef & cabbage, 52
Corned beef hash casserole, 9
Cornmeal topping, 43
Corn pie, chile, with fresh tomato salsa, 43
Corn with tomato-cheese topping, baked, 83
Cottage sauce, sour, 65
Crab & onion pie, 30
Crab & spaghetti bake, 30
Crab-stuffed chicken breasts, 16
Cracked wheat pilaf, 91
Cream enchiladas, chicken, 45
Creole, beef tongue, 10
Crêpes
basic, 56
chicken & artichoke, 56
ham & vegetable, 57
layered spinach & sausage, 8
spinach onion, 57
tomato seafood, 57
Crowd pleasers, 28-29
Crunchy zucchini & carrots, 90
Crusty fettucine puff, 10
Cumin rice with pine nuts, 92
Curried squash bake, 89
Curry, ground beef, 68
Custard squares, cheese & artichoke, 35
Custard squares, spinach & artichoke, 88

Deep-dish pizzas, 41
Dijon, chicken, 16
Dill & cheese bread, 86
Dumplings, for chicken, 19

Dumplings & chicken, 17

Easy meatballs, for meatball
    Stroganoff with peppers, 60
Egg & chile puff, 35
Egg pastry, for English beef &
    kidney pie, 53
Eggplant enchiladas, 32
Enchiladas
    beef & bean, 44
    chicken cream, 45
    eggplant, 32
    stacked cheese, 32
English beef & kidney pie, 52
Extraordinary tuna & noodle
    casserole, 25

Fettucine puff, crusty, 10
Fiesta tamale pie, 45
Fila chicken & artichoke
    casserole, 11
Finnan haddie & mushroom
    casserole, 78
Fish & celery root ramekins, 22
Fish bake, savory, 24
Fish fillets, cheese-topped, 64
Fish fillets Italiano, 64
Fish stew with spicy hot
    mayonnaise, 78
Florentine, salmon, 30
Florentine, sole, 67
Florentine turkey rolls, 21
Fontina white sauce, for
    seafood-stuffed pasta
    shells, 27
Freezing casseroles, tips for, 76
French loaf, meatball-
    stuffed, 70
Fresh tomato salsa, for chile
    corn pie, 43
Frittata, puffy sprout, 36

Garlic chicken, oven-
    sautéed, 20
Garlic lamb meatballs with
    lemon sauce, 29
Garlic-tomato zucchini bake, 89
Garnishing tricks, 14-15
Gingered carrots, 83
Glazed onions for boeuf
    bourguignon, 54
Goulash, Hungarian, 53
Greek meatballs with yogurt
    sauce, 60
Green beans in Swiss cheese
    sauce, 80
Green beans Oriental, 81
Green beans supreme, 80
Green chile strata & sausage, 8
Green vegetable rice, 92
Ground beef curry, 68

Ham, spinach & brown rice, 9
Ham & pea pasta ramekins, 9
Ham & vegetable crêpes, 57
Hash, casserole, corned beef, 9
Hearty beef & bean stew, 4
Herb-cheese biscuits, for
    chicken ramekins, 77
Herb corn bread, 86
Herbed lamb shanks, 72
Herbed mushrooms, 84
Herb vegetable pie, 40

Huachinango, 46
Hungarian goulash, 53

Joe's special, 70

Kidney & beef pie, English, 52
Kotleti, baked, 51

Lamb
    & brown rice casserole, 72
    cassoulet, 54
    English beef & kidney pie, 52
    Greek meatballs with yogurt
        sauce, 60
    meatballs, garlic, with lemon
        sauce, 29
    moussaka Dubrovnik, 48
    ragout, savory, 61
    shanks, herbed, 72
    shanks, orange-flavored, 72
Lamb & brown rice
    casserole, 72
Lasagne, vegetarian's, 38
Lasagne belmonte, 51
Lattice-style crust, how to
    make, 15
Lattice-topped chicken pie, 12
Layered chile chicken &
    tortillas, 11
Layered spinach & sausage
    crêpes, 8
Lemon chicken, 62
Lentils & sausage casserole, 8
Lentils in tomato sauce,
    spicy, 93
Lentils with cheese, baked, 43
Limas, cheesy baked, 82

Macaroni & cheese,
    red hot, 37
Manicotti, cheese &
    mushroom, 37
Marinated onions, baked, 84
Meatball dinner, Oriental, 70
Meatballs, garlic lamb, with
    lemon sauce, 29
Meatball Stroganoff with
    peppers, 60
Meatball-stuffed French loaf, 70
Meatballs with yogurt sauce,
    Greek, 60
Mexican baked chicken, 20
Mexican rice with tomatoes, 93
Mixed grain pilaf, 78
Moussaka Dubrovnik, 48
Mushroom, artichoke &
    chicken casserole, 12
Mushroom & cheese
    manicotti, 37
Mushroom & finnan haddie
    casserole, 78
Mushroom-onion filling, for
    deep-dish pizzas, 43
Mushrooms, herbed, 84
Mushrooms & beef,
    biscuit-topped, 5
Mushroom soufflé,
    cheese-crusted, 33
Mushroom-wine sauce, 65

Noodle & tuna casserole,
    extraordinary, 25
Noodles, poppy seed, with beef
    Stroganoff, 53
Noodles, with oven short
    ribs, 6
Nut-raisin bread, 86

Olive & artichoke soufflé, 33
Onion & crab pie, 30
Onion-mushroom filling, for
    deep-dish pizzas, 43
Onions, baked marinated, 84
Onion spinach crêpes, 57
Orange chicken with carrots, 61
Orange-flavored lamb
    shanks, 72
Orange sauce, chicken breasts
    in, 13
Oriental chicken, 62
Oriental green beans, 81
Oriental meatball dinner, 70
Osso buco, 51
Oven-sautéed garlic chicken, 20
Oven short ribs with noodles, 6
Oven sweet & sour pork, 7

Paella, 46
Paprika chicken, baked, 19
Parmesan, asparagus, 80
Parmesan turkey steak, 22
Parsley cheese rice, 92
Pasta & cheese, sausage-
    stuffed, 7
Pasta ramekins, ham & pea, 9
Pasta shells, seafood-stuffed, 27
Pastitsio, 48
Pastry dough, for pies, 38, 40
Pea & celery medley, 88
Pea & ham pasta ramekins, 9
Peaches & chicken, spiced, 20
Peas & turkey, almond, 69
Peppers, with meatball
    Stroganoff, 60
Pesto sauce, for veal scaloppine
    with teleme, 29
Pie
    Chilean corn & chicken, 21
    chile corn, with fresh tomato
        salsa, 43
    crab & onion, 30
    English beef & kidney, 52
    fiesta tamale, 45
    lattice-topped chicken, 12
    ratatouille cheese, 38
    Swiss chard & cheese, 40
    tuna spaghetti, 25
    vegetable herb, 40
Pilaf
    chicken & rice, 77
    classic, 90
    cracked wheat vegetable, 91
    mixed grain, 91
Pine nuts, with cumin rice, 92
Piperade with bacon &
    vegetables, 68
Pizzas, deep-dish, 41
Poached chicken, for fila
    chicken & artichoke
    casserole, 12
Polynesian shrimp & rice, 25

Poppy seed noodles, with beef
    Stroganoff, 53
Pork
    arroz con pollo, 44
    biscuit-topped chicken
        ramekins, 75
    with brown rice & vegetables,
        barbecued, 77
    cassoulet, 54
    corned beef hash casserole, 9
    crusty fettucine puff, 10
    fiesta tamale pie, 45
    green chile strata & sausage, 8
    ham, spinach & brown rice, 9
    ham & pea pasta ramekins, 9
    ham & vegetable crêpes, 57
    layered spinach & sausage
        crêpes, 8
    lentils & sausage casserole, 8
    meatball-stuffed French
        loaf, 70
    Moussaka Dubrovnik, 48
    Oriental meatball dinner, 70
    paella, 46
    piperade with bacon &
        vegetables, 68
    potato-sausage supper, 68
    saffron spaghetti bake, 7
    sausages with sauerkraut, 52
    sausage-stuffed pasta &
        cheese, 7
    sweet & sour, oven, 7
    veal Stroganoff, 73
Potato caraway bread, 87
Potatoes & carrots, with
    chicken, 19
Potatoes Anna, 85
Potatoes au gratin, 84
Potato loaf, browned, 85
Potato salad casserole, 84
Potato-sausage supper, 68
Pot au feu, 59
Puffy sprout frittata, 36

Quick sole & shrimp
    casserole, 24

Raclette, Rocky Mountain, 85
Ragout, savory lamb, 61
Raisin-nut bread, 86
Ratatouille cheese pie, 38
Red hot macaroni & cheese, 37
Rice, confetti, 92
Rice, green vegetable, 92
Rice, parsley cheese, 92
Rice & broccoli casserole, 82
Rice & carrot casserole, 83
Rice & cheese stuffing, with
    Swiss chard, 37
Rice & shrimp, Polynesian, 25
Rice pilaf & chicken, 77
Rice with pine nuts, cumin, 92
Rice with tomatoes,
    Mexican, 93
Risotto, 91
Rocky Mountain raclette, 85
Rum-baked beans, 81

Saffron spaghetti bake, 7
Salmon Florentine, 30

Salsa, fresh tomato, for chile corn pie, 43
Salsa, with brown rice-vegetable casserole, 36
Sauces for the diet-conscious cook, 65
Sauerkraut, savory, 88
Sauerkraut, with beef cabbage rolls, 6
Sauerkraut, with sausages, 52
Sausage & green chile strata, 8
Sausage & lentils casserole, 8
Sausage & spinach crêpes, layered, 8
Sausage, potato supper, 68
Sausage-stuffed pasta & cheese, 7
Sausages with sauerkraut, 52
Savory beef stew, 4
Savory chicken in white wine, 17
Savory fish bake, 24
Savory lamb ragout, 61
Savory sauerkraut, 88
Scallopine, veal, with teleme, 28
Seafood
 cheese-topped fish fillets, 64
 cod with capers, baked, 27
 coquilles St. Jacques, 59
 crab & onion pie, 30
 crab & spaghetti bake, 30
 finnan haddie & mushroom casserole, 78
 fish & celery root ramekins, 22
 fish fillets Italiano, 64
 fish stew with spicy hot mayonnaise, 78
 huachinango, 46
 paella, 46
 salmon Florentine, 30
 savory fish bake, 24
 seafood-stuffed pasta shells, 27
 shrimp & rice, Polynesian, 25
 shrimp with wild rice, 67
 sole Florentine, 67
 sole & shrimp casserole, quick, 24
 sole in wine sauce, 24
 tomato seafood crêpes, 57
 tuna & noodle casserole, extraordinary, 25
 tuna spaghetti pie, 25
Sesame chicken in tarragon cream, 19
Short ribs with noodles, oven, 6
Shrimp & rice, Polynesian, 25
Shrimp & sole casserole, quick, 24
Shrimp with wild rice, 67
Sicilian beef & vegetable casserole, 5
Skillet Stroganoff, 73
Sole & shrimp casserole, quick, 24
Sole Florentine, 67
Sole in wine sauce, 24
Soufflé
 artichoke & olive, 33
 broccoli, with cheese sauce, 35

Soufflé (cont'd.)
 Camembert, 33
 carrot, 83
 cheese-crusted mushroom, 33
Sour cottage sauce, 65
Sour cream biscuits, for beef & mushrooms, 5
Spaghetti & crab bake, 30
Spaghetti saffron bake, 7
Spaghetti tuna pie, 25
Spiced chicken & peaches, 20
Spicy hot mayonnaise, for fish stew, 78
Spicy lentils in tomato sauce, 93
Spicy marinara sauce, for Swiss chard with rice & cheese stuffing, 37
Spinach, brown rice & ham, 9
Spinach & artichoke custard squares, 88
Spinach & artichokes au gratin, 88
Spinach & sausage crêpes, layered, 8
Spinach & squash casserole, 41
Spinach onion crêpes, 57
Spinach-stuffed chicken breasts, 75
Sprout frittata, puffy, 36
Squash & spinach casserole, 41
Squash bake, curried, 89
Stacked cheese enchiladas, 32
Stew, fish, with spicy hot mayonnaise, 78
Stew, savory beef, 4
Stew, stovetop beef, 73
Stovetop beef stew, 73
Strata, green chile & sausage, 8
Stroganoff, beef, with poppy seed noodles, 53
Stroganoff, meatball, with peppers, 60
Stroganoff, skillet, 73
Stroganoff, veal, 73
Supreme green beans, 80
Sweet & sour pork, oven, 7
Sweet & sour sauce, for turkey patties, 70
Sweet & sour turkey patties, 69
Swiss chard & cheese pie, 40
Swiss chard with rice & cheese stuffing, 37
Swiss cheese sauce, green beans in, 80

Tamale pie, fiesta, 45
Tarragon chicken, 13
Tarragon cream, sesame chicken in, 19
Tartar sauce, 65
Teleme, with veal scaloppine, 28
Tetrazzini, chicken, 49
Three wheat batter bread, 87
Tips for freezing & transporting casseroles, 76
Tomato-cheese topping, with baked corn, 83
Tomatoes, with Mexican rice, 93
Tomatoes, zucchini-stuffed, 89

Tomato-garlic zucchini bake, 89
Tomato-mushroom sauce, for sausage-stuffed pasta & cheese, 7
Tomato salsa, fresh, for chile corn pie, 43
Tomato sauce, for deep-dish pizzas, 41
Tomato sauce, for veal scaloppine with teleme, 28
Tomato sauce, spicy lentils in, 93
Tomato seafood crêpes, 57
Tongue creole, beef, 10
Tortilla & turkey casserole, 21
Tortillas & chile chicken, layered, 11
Transporting casseroles, tips for, 76
Tuna & noodle casserole, extraordinary, 25
Tuna spaghetti pie, 25
Turkey
 legs & vegetables, baked, 64
 patties, sweet & sour, 69
 & peas, almond, 69
 rolls, Florentine, 21
Turkey & tortilla casserole, 21
Turkey steak Parmesan, 22

Veal
 meatball Stroganoff with peppers, 60
 osso buco, 51
Veal scaloppine with teleme, 28
Veal Stroganoff, 73
Vegetable & beef casserole, Sicilian, 5
Vegetable & ham crêpes, 57
Vegetable barley casserole, 93

Vegetable-brown rice casserole with salsa, 36
Vegetable cracked wheat pilaf, 91
Vegetable herb pie, 40
Vegetable rice, green, 92
Vegetables & bacon, with piperade, 68
Vegetables & brown rice, with barbecued pork, 77
Vegetables & chicken in wine, 61
Vegetables & turkey legs, baked, 64
Vegetarian's lasagne, 38

Wheat batter bread, three, 87
White wine, savory chicken in, 17
Wild rice, with shrimp, 67
Wine, chicken & vegetables in, 61
Wine, white, savory chicken in, 17
Wine, with classic chicken, 75
Wine-mushroom sauce, 65
Wine sauce, sole in, 24

Yam & cashew casserole, 90
Yogurt sauce, for Greek meatballs, 61
Yorkshire relleno, 6

Zucchini & carrots, crunchy, 90
Zucchini-artichoke filling, for deep-dish pizzas, 41
Zucchini bake, tomato-garlic, 89
Zucchini-stuffed tomatoes, 89

Handy Metric Conversion Table

To change	To	Multiply by
ounces (oz.)	grams (g)	28
pounds (lbs.)	kilograms (kg)	0.45
teaspoons	milliliters (ml)	5
tablespoons	milliliters (ml)	15
fluid ounces (fl. oz.)	milliliters (ml)	30
cups	liters (l)	0.24
pints (pt.)	liters (l)	0.47
quarts (qt.)	liters (l)	0.95
gallons (gal.)	liters (l)	3.8
inches	centimeters (cm)	2.5
Fahrenheit temperature (°F)	Celsius temperature (°C)	5/9 after subtracting 32